Perthshire
40 Town & Country Walks

The authors and publisher have made every effort to ensure that the information in this publication is accurate, and accept no responsibility whatsoever for any loss, injury or inconvenience experienced by any person or persons whilst using this book.

published by
pocket mountains ltd
The Old Church, Annanside, Moffat,
Dumfries and Galloway DG10 9HB
www.pocketmountains.com

ISBN: 978-1-916739-16-1

Text and photography copyright © Paul and Helen Webster
First published 2009, revised in new edition 2025

The right of Paul and Helen Webster to be identified as the Authors of this work has been asserted by them in accordance with the Copyright, Designs and Patents Act 1988

A catalogue record for this book is available from the British Library

Contains Ordnance Survey data © Crown copyright and database 2025

All rights reserved. No part of this publication may be reproduced, stored in a retrieval system, or transmitted in any form or by any means, electronic or mechanical, including photocopying and recording, unless expressly permitted by Pocket Mountains Ltd.

Printed by J Thomson Colour Printers, Glasgow

Introduction

Perthshire is at the very heart of Scotland, within easy reach of the cities of Glasgow and Edinburgh yet a world apart – offering a huge variety of scenery encompassing both Highland and Lowland landscapes. As well as the historic Fair City itself, Perthshire includes many attractive small towns – Pitlochry, Dunkeld, Crieff, Blairgowrie and Aberfeldy among them.

The mighty River Tay enjoys almost legendary status amongst salmon fishermen and it is just one of several fine rivers that carve their way through glens so richly wooded that the area has been branded 'Big Tree Country'. Remarkable trees include the Fortingall Yew – thought to be the oldest living organism in Europe – as well as the world's highest hedge, a contender for Britain's tallest tree and a surviving oak from Shakespeare's Birnam Wood. Above the trees are heather-clad hills and mountains – including lofty Ben Lawers and the graceful cone of Schiehallion, the Fairy Mountain.

A classic Perthshire image is that of the Highland castle, whether it be the dazzling white fairytale of Blair Castle, the dour fortress of Castle Menzies where Bonnie Prince Charlie stayed en route to Culloden or Scone Palace, where for many centuries the kings of Scotland were crowned on the Stone of Destiny. Other attractions include whisky distilleries (both Scotland's oldest and smallest are found here), historic gardens and golf courses, as well as events ranging from traditional Highland Games to music festivals and the Enchanted Forest, an annual extravaganza of music and lights.

This guide features 40 moderate walks in all parts of Perthshire and Kinross, including Killin near the head of Loch Tay, historically part of the region.

Safety and what to take

While some of the routes are waymarked, many others are not and the sketch maps accompanying them are intended as an aid to planning rather than navigation. It is recommended that you take – and know how to use – the relevant OS or Harvey map and compass.

Weather can be extreme on higher ground. The Ben Vrackie route, in particular, crosses high and exposed ground and, even at lower altitudes, the weather can change rapidly. It is always advisable to carry wind- and waterproof clothing and adequate warm layers to allow the walks to be completed safely if the weather does deteriorate. Most of the routes are suitable for families with children in good conditions and could be completed in stout walking shoes, but boots are recommended for the more exposed or rougher ground.

Access

Perth is served by railway lines from both Glasgow and Edinburgh, while a third line extends northwards through Highland Perthshire en route to Inverness.

Additionally, there are good bus services to most towns and villages throughout the region. Where a walk can be reached by public transport, it is indicated in the text.

The introduction of the Land Reform (Scotland) Act in 2003 gave walkers rights of access over most of Scotland away from residential buildings, but these rights entail responsibilities. Remember that much of the area is a working landscape, and always follow the Scottish Outdoor Access Code. In particular, keep dogs on tight leads during the spring and early summer and well away from sheep and lambs at all times. Stag stalking takes place on the hills mostly through September up to 20 October, but this would not usually conflict with routes on lower ground as described here.

History

Perthshire has a long and rich history. Although the Romans invaded this region under the leadership of Agricola, defeating the local Caledonian tribes at the Battle of Mons Graupius in 83AD, and later built a fort at Inchtuthil near Dunkeld, they were unable to subdue the tribesfolk for long and, after being subjected to a guerrilla campaign, retreated south. The best-known remains from this period are the crannogs, defensive loch dwellings, some of which date back to 5000BC. More than 20 such dwellings have been identified in Loch Tay alone, and there is an excellent reconstruction of one at the Scottish Crannog Centre near Kenmore.

Scone was the capital of the Kingdom of the Picts for many years while, further west, the Kingdom of the Gaels was centred on Dunadd in Argyll. Kenneth MacAlpin is traditionally claimed as the first king of Scotland and, according to legend, he brought the coronation stone, the Stone of Destiny, to Scone. Most modern historians believe it was his grandson Constantine, however, who truly united the two kingdoms when he overthrew a coup which had been carried out by a Gael, Giric. Constantine is thought to have defeated Giric at the hillfort of Dundurn above St Fillans. Whichever version of history is to be believed, Scone was the coronation place of the Scottish kings, and for several years it was also the seat of its parliament. When Edward I invaded Scotland he took the Stone of Destiny to Westminster, where, despite the Scots' eventual victory in the Wars of Independence, it remained in England until recent times.

The Glorious Revolution of 1688 saw the protestant William of Orange depose his uncle, the Catholic James II of England and VII of Scotland, to take the British throne. Many in northern Scotland were sympathetic to the exiled king and a series of uprisings in support of both James and his heirs wreaked havoc in the Highlands.

The first rising was led by John Graham who defeated the government forces at the Battle of Killiecrankie, just north of Pitlochry, in 1689, and was soon repressed. The next uprising was in 1715, led by the Earl of Mar in support of James Edward Stuart, the son of the deposed king. Within a fortnight of raising the standard near Braemar, Aberdeen, Montrose and Inverness had all fallen to the rebellion. The Earl of Mar himself occupied Perth with 5000 men. Mar was no military expert, though, and with his advance southwards blocked by fewer than 3000 government troops under the command of the Duke of Argyll from Blair Atholl, momentum was lost. Argyll received reinforcements before the eventual battle at Sheriffmuir, where both sides claimed victory but the Jacobites retreated to Perth. James Stuart briefly set up court at Scone, but eventually fled the country and his followers returned north.

In the aftermath of the rebellion, the government began an attempt to subdue the Highlands. Under General Wade, construction began on a series of forts and by 1730 he and his men had built a road from Dunkeld to Inverness, extending the existing route north from Perth. This was followed by a road connecting Crieff and the Dunkeld road via the Sma' Glen, creating a link with Stirling. The Tay was spanned by Wade's Bridge at Aberfeldy, the most expensive single structure on his entire road-building programme. Wade's efforts did not, however, prevent the second major uprising, led by Bonnie Prince Charlie in 1745. The Jacobites were eventually crushed at Culloden in 1746 and the Highlands repressed ruthlessly.

The clan system began to collapse as the remaining chiefs abandoned their role as guardian of their people and began instead to look for profits. The Industrial Revolution in the south was creating a massive demand for wool and the chiefs began to evict their tenants to make way for sheep. Perthshire did not escape the Highland Clearances entirely – with areas such as Glen Tilt and Glen Lednock largely emptied of people.

When the demand for wool declined, many estates turned to forestry. While the first commercial plantations were on Drummond Hill above Loch Tay, planted by Sir Duncan Campbell in the early 17th century, it was the Dukes of Atholl who began planting on a huge scale – around 27 million conifers in the 90 years to 1830.

Now, too, tourism began to take off, with deer-stalking, grouse-shooting and salmon-fishing the fashionable pastimes of Britain's elite, and writers such as Robert Burns, William Wordsworth and Sir Walter Scott were attracted to the area. Estate owners catered for such visitors by constructing follies, bridges and grottoes in places like the Hermitage near Dunkeld and the Falls of Acharn above Loch Tay. Rising incomes and improved transport slowly brought the region within the reach of the general public, and its popularity has continued to this day.

◀ Loch Faskally

The handsome stone-built town of Pitlochry has been one of the most popular resorts in the Highlands ever since Queen Victoria visited during her first trip to Scotland in 1842. Today, the town is perhaps best known for its Festival Theatre and for the salmon ladder beside the Faskally Dam, but it is the fine setting that draws visitors time and time again. The glens here are green, fertile and richly wooded, the mountains rounded and beckoning, and the rivers truly magnificent.

To the north, the Pass of Killiecrankie, which is now bypassed by the A9, leads through ancient woodland to the quieter village of Blair Atholl with its celebrated castle. The scenery here is more dramatic and Highland in character, with Glen Tilt stretching away as one of the most beautiful glens in all Scotland, accessible only on foot.

West of Pitlochry is Loch Tummel and the Queen's View. The landscape becomes progressively wilder and emptier on the approach to the lovely village of Kinloch Rannoch at the foot of Loch Rannoch. Looming above is the fairy mountain of Schiehallion, almost a perfect cone, before the road finally ends at the wilderness of Rannoch Station.

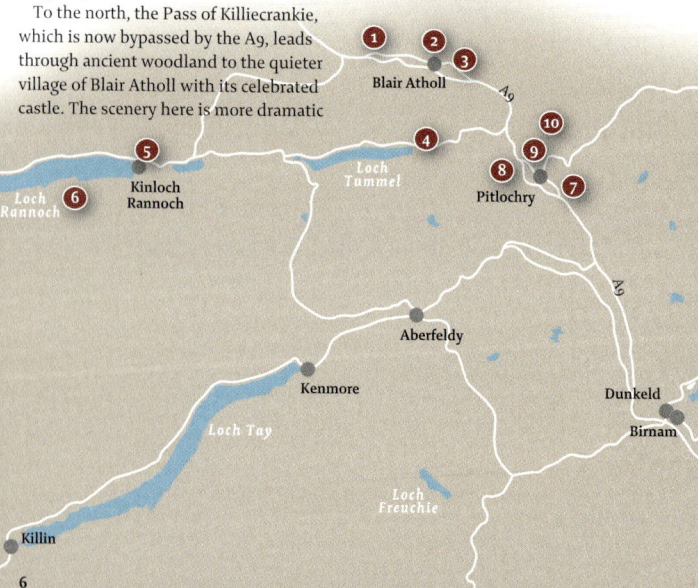

Pitlochry and North Perthshire

1 The Falls of Bruar 8
Follow in the poetic footsteps of
Robert Burns to a series of waterfalls
set in a delightful 'wild garden'

2 Glen Banvie and The Whim 10
Wind along a lovely glen to a folly
overlooking Blair Castle

3 Wilds of Glen Tilt 12
Venture into one of the wildest and
most beautiful glens in the Highlands

4 Allean Forest above Loch Tummel 14
Admire the royal view of this loch
before visiting a ruined blackhouse
and an ancient ring fort

5 Kinloch Rannoch and Craig Varr 16
Explore this tiny village in the
remotest part of Perthshire, with
a detour to a natural viewpoint

6 Loch Rannoch Forest Walk 18
Enjoy a quiet stroll through glades of
Scots pine above lonely Loch Rannoch

7 Black Spout and Edradour 20
Climb through woodland to pass
two historic distilleries and view an
enchanting waterfall

**8 Loch Faskally and the
Salmon Ladder** 22
Complete a lochside circuit from
Pitlochry, with a detour to Killiecrankie

9 Craigower over Pitlochry 24
Make your way up this wooded
crag which, though small, gives fine
views down Loch Tummel

10 Ben Vrackie 26
Tackle Pitlochry's mountain on this
exhilarating heather moorland climb

The Falls of Bruar

Distance 2.5km **Time** 1 hour 30
Terrain well-made path, steep sections with sheer drops **Map** OS Explorer OL49
Access bus to Bruar from Pitlochry

The series of cascades that make up the Falls of Bruar have been attracting visitors for more than 250 years. William Wordsworth and Queen Victoria both came here, as did Robert Burns in earlier times. This short but steep loop climbs upstream through pretty woodland with various viewpoints and bridges before returning down the opposite side. Although the path is clear, take care with children near the steep sides where there are vertical drops into the ravine.

The walk begins beside the House of Bruar shop and restaurant complex just north of Blair Atholl. A popular stopping point on the busy A9, the House of Bruar has built a reputation for quality products, including locally produced food. Start from the car park across the road from the House of Bruar buildings, cross the road and keep right and then left to follow the Bruar Water upstream with the back of the building to your left. The path passes under the Edinburgh-Inverness railway line and through a gate to follow an obvious route through the woods, with the river rushing through a series of deep pools far below.

People began to visit the falls as road construction opened up the area in the 1720s. On coming here, Robert Burns was moved by the bare hillsides to write 'The Humble Petition of Bruar Water' in which he pleaded with the 4th Duke of Atholl to clothe the barren slopes with 'lofty firs and ashes cool'. After Burns' death, the Duke began building the path network and

◀ Falls from the Lower Bridge

bridges as well as planting the first of the pines. These original plantations, begun around 1796, were mostly felled to provide wood during the Second World War. Planting resumed after the war to provide the mixture of pine, birch, rowan, aspen and willow that can be enjoyed today.

The path ahead passes a flight of wooden steps, which climbs up to a viewpoint on the right. This overlooks the first of the falls, with a rock arch across the riverbed as foreground. Continuing upstream, you come to the Lower Bridge where to the left you'll see an arch – the remains of a 'viewing house'. The early tourists liked to frame their views with arches or grottoes, often hiding them until the last moment for dramatic effect. Viewing houses were built with narrow entrances to provide sudden 'surprise' views of waterfalls and ravines. Do not cross the Lower Bridge yet, but instead continue on the now steep uphill path on the near side. Further up, ignore the path which climbs to the left away from the river. Eventually, you reach the Upper Bridge, handsomely built to enable the early visitors to appreciate the falls. Its situation gives beautiful views downstream and out over the unfolding Perthshire countryside.

Cross the bridge and follow the path on a rising course for a short distance. To the left is another path to a picnic area with a great outlook over the Bruar Water. The walk continues on the path as it curves to the right and begins its descent towards the Lower Bridge, passing a number of good vantage points over the falls along the way. When you reach the Lower Bridge, cross the water to rejoin the outward route, turning left to head back to the start of the walk.

Glen Banvie and The Whim

Distance 6km **Time** 2 hours
Terrain clear, waymarked track, minor road **Maps** OS Explorer OL49 and OL51
Access bus or train from Pitlochry to Blair Atholl, a short walk from the start

Follow the Banvie Burn past stone bridges and through a wooded glen to visit the charming settlement of Old Blair and the gothic arches of The Whim.

The walk starts at the well-signed car park near Old Bridge of Tilt. From Blair Atholl, follow the road north to Old Bridge of Tilt and left through the village, then cross the bridge to find the car park on the left. This approach can also be made on foot, which adds 3km to the round trip.

Leave the car park by the main entrance and turn left along the road. Bear right at the fork to follow the sloping road gently uphill. Go straight ahead at the crossroads onto a path, which passes a bungalow.

Keeping to the black arrows, fork left after the bungalow. As elsewhere in the Highlands, the Atholl Estate is battling against the spread of the pervasive rhododendron which, though planted here as an exotic species in the 18th century, has thrived to such an extent that it poses a serious threat to biodiversity – responding to hard pruning with equally aggressive growth. Red squirrels can sometimes be seen in the woods, but you're more likely to hear them scampering up and down the tree trunks.

When the path rejoins the track, bear left. Further on, bear left at a fork, soon reaching an old stone bridge over the burn. Instead of crossing here, continue on the track and bear left at the next fork to reach upper Banvie Bridge. During late summer, the open hillsides in front of you

GLEN BANVIE AND THE WHIM

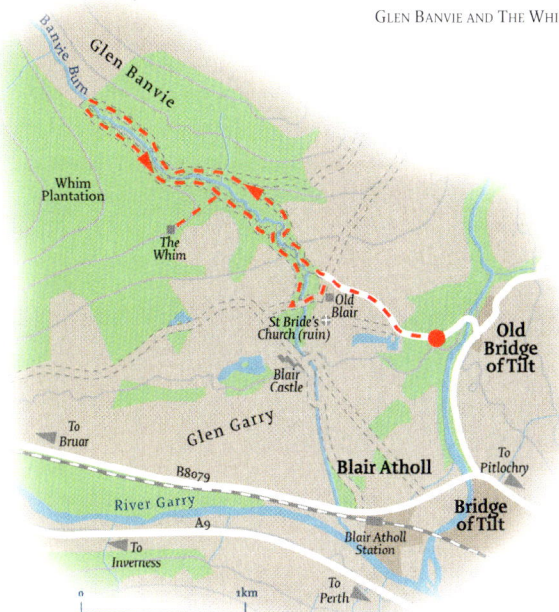

◀ The Whim

are ablaze with purple heather while in winter you may spot red deer sheltering on the edges of the wood.

Cross the bridge to begin the walk back down the far side of the burn. Carry straight on where the gently rising track is joined by another from the right, then bear left at the next fork to pass (and again not cross) the first bridge you encountered. Further on, you'll see a clear path off to the right. This is a short detour to The Whim, a stone-built folly consisting of three gothic arches. It was built in 1761 to give a focal point to the outlook from Blair Castle but also gives a beautiful view back to the castle and its landscaped grounds against the Perthshire hills. Return to the main track and carry on down the glen.

The track passes to the left of a house and then down an elegant avenue of trees to reach a minor road. Turn right if you wish to detour to the splendid castle (charge), which also has a restaurant (seasonal opening), or turn left and pass under a stone footbridge to reach the picturesque hamlet of Old Blair. Before heading left along the road, you can detour to the right to explore the ruins of St Bride's Church. Just beyond Old Blair is the crossroads: turn right here to return to the start.

Wilds of Glen Tilt

Distance 6km **Time** 2 hours 30
Terrain good tracks and paths
Maps OS Explorer OL49 and OL51
Access bus or train from Pitlochry to Blair Atholl, a short walk from the start

Glen Tilt is a real gem – all idyllic woods, clear, rushing water and lofty peaks. This route climbs to a magnificent viewpoint giving a taste of the upper glen before looping back through woodland above the gorge containing the River Tilt.

The walk starts from the car park just beyond the Old Bridge of Tilt. From Blair Atholl, follow the road north to Old Bridge of Tilt and turn left through the hamlet, then cross the bridge to find the car park on the left.

Leave the car park by the main entrance and turn left along the road. Very shortly, stone steps on the right offer the chance to detour up to the Balvenie Pillar which marks the spot where the last public hanging on the Atholl Estate took place in 1630. Return down to the road and keep right to follow it gently uphill. At a crossroads, turn right up a lane (signed Private Road) that leads you past a picturesque pair of estate cottages, ignoring another lane that branches right.

The road becomes a track as it passes the castellated farmhouse of Bailanloan below, with fine views down the glen. Passing Blairuachdar, the track is lined with splendid trees as it continues gradually climbing and heading round a sharp bend before entering the woods. Ignore a track coming in from the left. Where the route forks, keep on the lower right-hand track.

Further on, green waymarkers indicate a sharp right-hand turn onto a path heading downhill. This is the return route, but before going this way, carry on along the main track for about 300m for the

WILDS OF GLEN TILT

◀ Glen Tilt

stunning view up Glen Tilt from the entrance to a rifle range. Back in 1847, this glen was the scene of an encounter which led to the establishment of a right of way through the glen and the beginning of Scotland's access rights. John Balfour, a professor of botany at the University of Edinburgh, organised field studies for his students in the Highlands each summer. On one such trip down Glen Tilt, he found his way barred by the Duke of Atholl and his ghillies. A violent end to the stand-off was avoided when Balfour and his students climbed over a dyke and ran off, but a lengthy legal case ensued which eventually vindicated Balfour and led to the creation of the Scottish Rights of Way and Recreation Society. This is today known as ScotWays, a campaigning body on access issues which is also responsible for the small green signs pointing out rights of way in the Highlands, many of them ambitious cross-country walks.

Return to the junction to drop down through fine woodland on the track. After a steep section, this crosses a small bridge and makes the gentler descent through birchwoods before reaching the main track up Glen Tilt. Turn right along this. After 1.5km, a yellow arrow indicates an optional loop off to the left to view the Falls of Fender. The falls are often obscured by foliage and are less impressive than they once were due to the extraction of water for hydro-electric schemes, but the loop is worthwhile for its woodland scenery alone. Rejoin the track and carry on until another path (not waymarked) goes off to the left. Turn left here and descend to cross a stone bridge over the road near the Old Bridge of Tilt before taking the steep path up to the right (red arrow) to return to the car park.

13

Allean Forest above Loch Tummel

Distance 4km **Time** 1 hour 30
Terrain clear paths and forest track
Map OS Explorer OL49 **Access** bus from
Pitlochry to Queen's View Visitor Centre,
a short walk from the start

A gentle forest walk above Loch Tummel, beginning near the famous Queen's View. The walk has its own viewpoint over the loch as well as a restored blackhouse and the remains of a ring fort.

The Queen's View is a deservedly popular stopping place. Almost the whole length of Loch Tummel is framed by beautiful slopes and the distinctive peak of Schiehallion; on perfect days, even the mountains of Glencoe can be picked out in the far distance. Queen Victoria came here by carriage in 1866, though the name may hark back to an earlier visit by Queen Isabella, wife of Robert the Bruce. Today, there is a café and visitor centre at the viewpoint car park.

This walk actually begins from the Allean Forest car park (charge), just along the road toward Kinloch Rannoch from the Queen's View, where there are picnic tables and composting toilets. Take the marked trail uphill past the long-drop toilets – which may be an attraction in itself for some green-minded visitors – and over a bridge into the pinewoods. When the path emerges onto a track, turn left to follow the red and yellow marker posts. Soon the route turns right onto another track before plunging left into the forest on the opposite side. This path leads over a small bridge and along a section carpeted with wood anemone, foxgloves and sorrel in spring and summer to emerge in a clearing where you'll find a partially restored blackhouse. This building would have been typical of

◀ Loch Tummel

the village, or *clachan* in Gaelic, with stone walls, a roof of turf or heather, and few windows. There was no chimney, so the walls would have been coated in soot – hence the name – and it would have been home to an entire family. After passing the house, a marker post directs you away from the information board to the left.

Further on, a short detour takes you to a lovely wooden sculpture, though the view over Loch Tummel from here is now obscured by trees. Back on the path, cross a wooden bridge and then a track by a short dog-leg to the left. The route now climbs, with views of the surrounding countryside. When this joins a track, head left downhill and ignore a path with a yellow waymarker on the right. Where the main track curves left, take the right branch with a red marker post. This narrows to a path once again before meeting another track, where you turn right to shortly reach a sign for the ring fort. Here are the remains of a large circular Iron Age roundhouse or ring fort. The earth and stone walls may have once held a roof, supported by wooden poles. Despite the name, ring forts were not primarily defensive structures – and this part of Perthshire has the best remaining examples. After enjoying the peaceful views over Loch Tummel from here, continue downhill by the track to meet the T-junction encountered earlier in the walk. Turn left to return to the car park and the start.

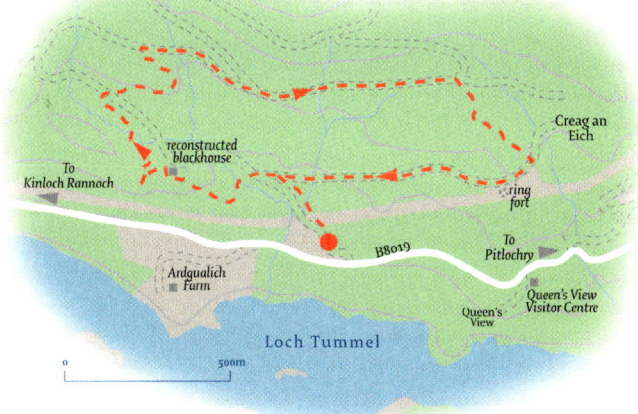

Kinloch Rannoch and Craig Varr

Distance 4km (+4km detour) **Time** 1 hour (+2 hour detour) **Terrain** waymarked forest paths and tracks, fairly level; steep ascent on optional detour followed by open ground with some rough sections **Map** OS Explorer OL49 **Access** bus to Kinloch Rannoch from Pitlochry

This short walk explores the picturesque village of Kinloch Rannoch, a gateway to one of the wilder areas of Scotland, with an optional steep climb to a fantastic natural viewpoint over the village and Loch Rannoch.

At the foot of Loch Rannoch, Kinloch Rannoch is an attractive village seemingly set in the middle of nowhere. The road to the west now terminates at Rannoch Station, but in years gone by the route continued across the barren landscapes of Rannoch Moor and beyond – as this was the famous Road to the Isles. The walk starts in the attractive square at the centre of the village where there is some parking. Head along the road in the direction of Pitlochry, passing an industrial building on your left. Just beyond, turn left after a fence to head up a footpath beside a stone cottage signposted for Craig Varr. Carry on through a gate to pass a waterfall and continue up to the hydro building on the left. Continue for a short distance to where the path forks.

The path up the hill marks the start of the steep and rough ascent of Craig Varr, with its sensational views over Loch Rannoch and the surrounding mountains. This strenuous detour winds up through the woods; when you reach open ground turn right at a fork to cross a bridge. Keep to the obvious route until just beyond a gate, turning left here to follow a fence and then stone dyke across boggy ground to the prow of Craig Varr. Return the same way.

To miss out the detour, turn left where the Craig Varr path heads uphill and

Kinloch Rannoch and Craig Varr

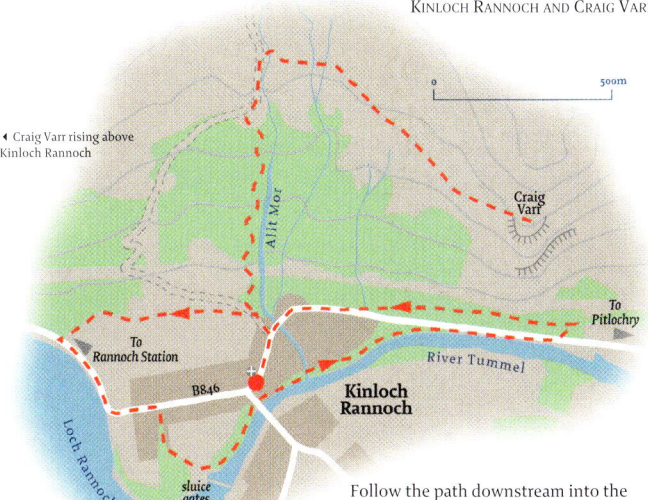

◂ Craig Varr rising above Kinloch Rannoch

follow the path marked for Loch Rannoch. This runs just above the fields, with good views over the village. Beyond a stone well, the path shadows the drystane dyke before emerging by houses onto a tarmac road. Turn left to follow this as it curves around the shores of Loch Rannoch.

After a sharp left bend, you come to the edge of the village. Turn right onto a track just after the first cottage and immediately left through a gate. Fork left again by the electricity substation onto a small path. This leads to the sluice gates at the foot of Loch Rannoch. The loch is part of the huge Tummel hydro-power scheme, which was constructed in the 1930s and uses water from all the surrounding glens. The powerful flow of the river is controlled and can rise and fall very quickly.

Follow the path downstream into the woods and pass under the stone bridge. A left turn here leads back into the village but this walk continues beside the river. Eventually the path bends left to reach a footbridge. Turn right to cross this and pass to the right of some houses. When the surfaced path curves left, fork right to leave it, taking a path through the woods. This soon rejoins the river on its journey downstream, before ending after a parking area to emerge on the road. Cross this and go through the gate directly opposite, signed for the Hillside Path. As soon as possible, turn very sharp left onto a beautiful path that rises through the edge of the woods, heading back towards the village amongst magnificent trees. Go through a gate and then fork left onto a path that leads down into Kinloch Rannoch. Turn right when you reach the road to return to the start.

Loch Rannoch Forest Walk

Distance 8km **Time** 2 hours 30
Terrain clear, waymarked forest paths and tracks **Map** OS Explorer 385
Access no public transport to the start

This waymarked circuit combines easy walking on forest tracks with pleasant mixed woodland, including remnants of the ancient Caledonian forest, with good views over Loch Rannoch.

The walk sets out from the Forestry and Land Scotland car park at Carie on the south side of Loch Rannoch. From the far end of the car park, head for the wooden footbridge over the falls. Do not cross, but instead follow the multicoloured marker posts along the path away from the bridge. Before reaching the picnic tables and large shelter, turn right for a gentle climb, then right again at the next junction. The path now climbs through the trees until it reaches a cross-paths. Turn left here to pass pine trees on the left and more open woodland on the right. At another junction, follow the yellow marker post and bear right.

After the Jacobite rebellions of 1690, 1715 and 1745, vast Highland estates were forfeited by their chiefs and seized by the crown as punishment for support of the rebel cause. The Forfeited Estates Commission was established to oversee this land and at Carie the commission operated its own sawmill to harvest the timber from the Black Wood of Rannoch.

The track rises gently until it is high above the Allt na Bogair, which can be glimpsed through the trees on the left as it tumbles towards Loch Rannoch. Parts of the forest floor are exposed to the sunlight here, and blaeberry and bracken flourish in thick clumps at the side of the

LOCH RANNOCH FOREST WALK

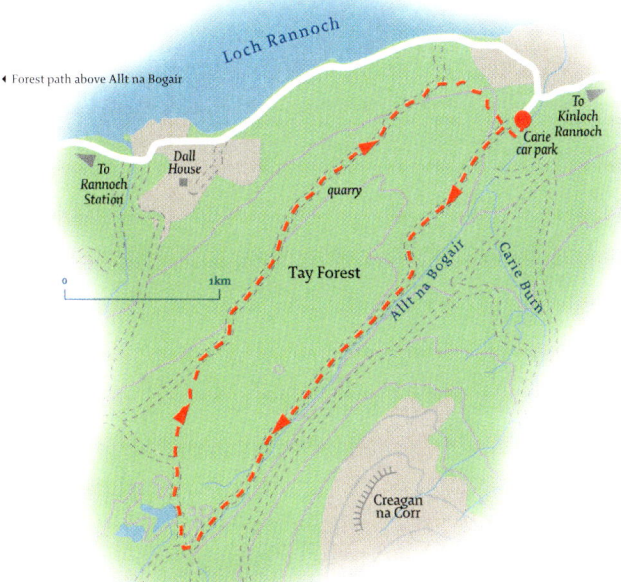

◀ Forest path above Allt na Bogair

path whilst majestic stands of Scots pine tower above. On this section, you'll spy a waterfall far below; the banks are very steep. After a while, the path drops down to the water. Continue on the path as it heads up to the right and joins a wide forestry track.

Turn right along this track. (To the left is an isolated route that leads to Glen Lyon via the Lairig Ghallabhaich. It gives a fantastic feeling of remoteness – but hillwalking gear is necessary, as well as transport at the far end.) The track leads past a forest lochan; soon after it swings left – go straight ahead here along a narrow path waymarked in yellow, before emerging at another track. Bear right here for a gradual descent, passing a small quarry on the right. To the left, there are glimpses of Loch Rannoch and the empty hills beyond.

After just over 2km on the track, keep an eye out for the next turning onto the yellow-waymarked path to the right. Marked by two small cairns, the path climbs to a sculpted seat with a superb view over Loch Rannoch. Eventually it drops to rejoin the outward path at the cross-paths. Go straight ahead here and then left at the next junction to return to the car park at the start.

Black Spout and Edradour

Distance 5km **Time** 2 hours
Terrain woodland paths, minor road, tracks, main road with pavement
Map OS Explorer OL49 **Access** Pitlochry is well served by buses, coaches and trains

This varied walk begins from the centre of Pitlochry, rising through woodland to view Black Spout waterfall and pass the Edradour Distillery, a huddle of pretty whitewashed buildings, with good views of the River Tummel and surrounding hills on the return.

Set off from the Atholl Road car park (charge) on the main street of Pitlochry. (There is also a smaller car park at the start of the path into Black Spout Wood.) Facing away from the car park, turn left and follow the main road towards Dunkeld. Where the road passes under the railway line, cross to the opposite side of the road to use the underpass and then back again. After passing the Blair Atholl Distillery and a row of bungalows, turn left uphill, signposted for Black Spout Wood, and pass back under the railway. Keeping to the track on the left, enter the woods for a gentle ascent, with the Atholl Palace Hotel golf putting course over to the left.

Now on a path at a crossroads, the yellow marker for Edradour directs you straight on, eventually bringing you to the Black Spout viewpoint. The river plunges vertically for more than 60m here: the falls are particularly dramatic after heavy rainfall.

The footpath now takes you on a winding uphill course: keep to the yellow marker posts and stay right at a fork. After

◂ Black Spout

climbing to a stone wall, the path runs along the edge of some fields with good views over to Ben Vrackie on the left.

After passing a stone cottage, you emerge just to the left of the pretty distillery complex of Edradour. The machinery and stills have remained almost unchanged since the distillery was built in the early 19th century.

Turn left up the road and follow this briefly to find a farm gate just before a set of ornamental stone gateposts on the left. From here, an enclosed, marked path skirts the edge of the field and passes a house, with fine views over Pitlochry as it starts to descend. Where it joins a grassy path, turn left for Pitlochry. By a house, the route re-enters Black Spout Wood and soon meets a larger track. Turn right here to head downhill, ignoring the slightly earlier path for Milton. In a very short while, at a wide bend, your path branches off to the right (identified by another yellow marker for Pitlochry). The path winds through the trees to reach a T-junction; turn right and soon descend to cross a wooden bridge and then bear left along the banks of the Kinnaird Burn.

Ignore the first path up to the right which leads to the imposing Atholl Palace Hotel but take the second one to head up to a road. Turn left to descend to the A924, passing the gatehouse at the entrance to the Atholl Palace Hotel. At the main road, turn right along the pavement to return to the start at the car park.

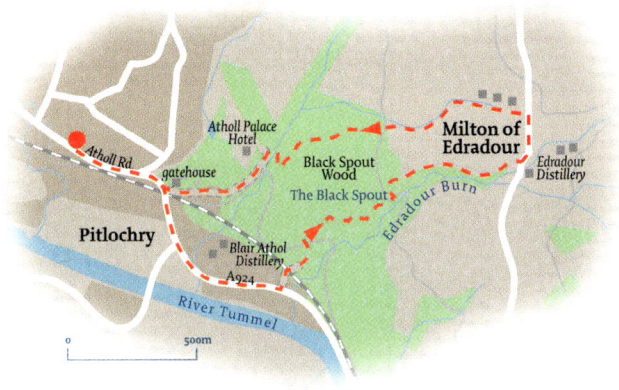

Loch Faskally and the Salmon Ladder

Distance 5km **Time** 2 hours **Terrain** good paths, flights of steps, minor roads
Map OS Explorer OL49 **Access** Pitlochry is well served by buses, coaches and trains

Combine a tour of Pitlochry's landmarks, including its well-known suspension bridge, Festival Theatre, salmon ladder and dam visitor centre, with a loop of Loch Faskally and an option to continue to historic Killiecrankie.

Start from the centre of Pitlochry by the war memorial at the junction of the main street (Atholl Road) and Ferry Road. Walk down Ferry Road, past the memorial gardens and under the railway, curving left to pass a restaurant.

Immediately after the sports field, turn left down a path (signposted for the Festival Theatre and the Fish Ladder) to find the Port-na-Craig Suspension Bridge. Cross this and turn right along the road, passing the Port-na-Craig Inn and the Festival Theatre. Today's famous theatre started life in a large tent in 1951. The current building opened in 1981 and, as well as a full season of plays, it has a popular café, shop and gardens.

Carry on along the minor road towards the hydro-electric dam, which created Loch Faskally in 1951. An Act of Parliament required the Hydro Board to preserve fish stocks on any waterways affected by the scheme, hence the fish ladder seen on the left side of the dam. It consists of 34 tiered pools with interconnected openings below the waterline to allow fish to swim up into the next pool, and two larger 'rest' pools.

The steps just beyond the information boards lead to the top of the dam. Keep left up a few more steps for the circuit of Loch Faskally. At a fork, go right to drop

◀ Shores of Loch Faskally

down some steps to the shore, where a clear path skirts the water's edge with one deviation down and then up a long flight of steps to cross a bridge. The path soon leaves the water and approaches the thunderingly busy A9. Stay in the woods to eventually pass a house at Balmore and meet a minor road, which you accompany gently downhill to the right. After passing under the A9 bridge, take an immediate right over a footbridge with good views to the left where the loch widens again.

If you wish to detour along the rest of the loch and the River Garry to Killiecrankie and the famous Soldier's Leap (5km), turn left here and follow the green waymarkers, keeping the water on your left. The path eventually leads to the visitor centre, where you can catch a bus for the 10-minute ride back to Pitlochry; check the timetable first.

For the main route, turn right on the far side of the bridge, passing back under the A9. After the boating station and café, go straight on to join a road which climbs past the Green Park Hotel. Turn right after the hotel and head into a small housing estate. When the road bends left take the path on your right to go straight down to the lochside, passing through lovely woodland. Keep to the main path nearest the water, ignoring any tracks coming in from the left.

Follow the path as it reaches and skirts around the Pitlochry Dam Visitor Centre, well worth a visit to see the dramatic viewing platform, and learn more about hydro projects and how salmon navigate the fish ladder. The centre also has a café and toilets. Facing the front of the visitor centre, take the path on the left to descend the woodland steps, before emerging at an open grassy area. The route leads between the river and houses, turning left when you arrive back at the suspension bridge. Turn left here to retrace your steps to the town centre.

Craigower over Pitlochry

Distance 5km **Time** 2 hours
Terrain clear paths, steep at times
Map OS Explorer OL49 **Access** bus from Pitlochry to Moulin, 1.5km away; Pitlochry is well served by buses, coaches and trains

This short walk takes as its objective a wooded summit 400m above Pitlochry, a superb spot with wide-ranging views to Loch Tummel, Rannoch and, on a clear day, even the peaks of Glencoe. It is also a locally important habitat for butterflies.

The route starts from the small car park at Craigower, and is waymarked. Access by car is via the A924 northbound from Pitlochry, turning left immediately after the Moulin Inn to follow the road round to the small parking area at Balnacraig. To walk from Pitlochry itself, which adds 3km to the round trip, climb Larchwood Road, passing a former curling pond known as The Cuilc and then the golf clubhouse. At the top of the road, turn left to reach the parking area.

Begin the walk along the track (a continuation of the road) that leads past Balnacraig Steading to the golf course. Cross this, bearing right at the fork and keeping a watchful eye out for golf balls as you head up the path across the fairway to reach the fourth tee. There are great views from here back over the fine stone houses of Pitlochry and the countryside around it. A sign guides you left on a path along the

top edge of the golf course initially before diving into the woods for a gentle climb.

From the top of Craigower there are views over Pitlochry and to Loch Tummel and the iconic peak of Schiehallion. It was the regular shape and isolated position of Schiehallion that gave it its place in history as the spot where contour lines were invented. In 1774, Nevil Maskelyne, the Astronomer Royal, became the first to measure the mass of the earth, which he did by observing the deflection of a pendulum by the mass of Schiehallion. As part of the experiment, the volume of Schiehallion had to be calculated, for which purpose contours were invented by the geologist Charles Hutton, and have been used ever since to represent landscapes on 2D maps.

The waymarked central path continues briefly downhill, then swings right, with a climb up a couple of steps to join a forest track. Turn right along this, passing a communications mast as you meander steadily downhill. At a junction, turn left to rejoin the outward path through the woods and across the golf course to the start of the walk.

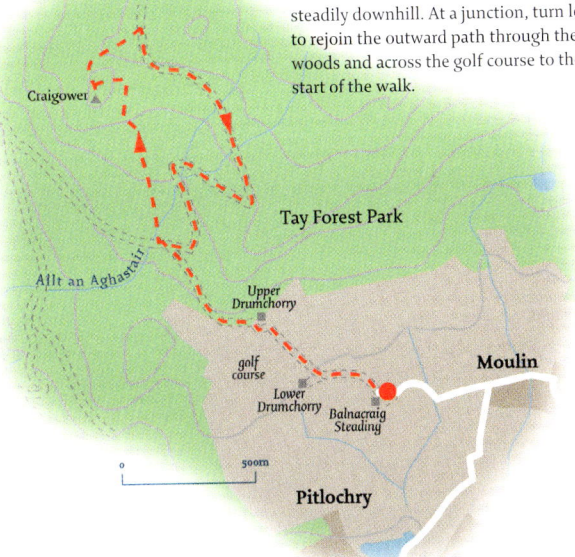

◀ Looking back over the golf course towards Pitlochry

PITLOCHRY AND NORTH PERTHSHIRE

Ben Vrackie

Distance 8.5km **Time** 4 hours
Terrain good hill path with a steep ascent to the summit; hillwalking gear is needed
Map OS Explorer OL49 **Access** bus from Pitlochry to Moulin, 1.5km away, then 500m walk along Baledmund Road

Ben Vrackie is the small mountain that is indelibly associated with Pitlochry: on a clear day, the views are magnificent. This route takes in woods, moorland and a pretty lochan with a final, steep climb and an optional 2km loop. The upper sections are exposed, so full hillwalking clothing, map and compass are essential.

Ben Vrackie's name, meaning 'Speckled Mountain' in Gaelic, is attributed to the vibrant mix of heather and grey stone on its flanks. At 841m high, it is classed as one of the 222 Scottish Corbetts, which are growing in popularity as an objective for walkers who have completed or want an alternative to the higher Munros. Ben Vrackie is easier than most and appeals to a much wider range of walkers.

There is a car park at the start of the walk which is just northwest of Moulin, 1.5km from Pitlochry. To reach this, turn left off the A924 just behind the Moulin Hotel and follow the road uphill, continuing straight ahead when it goes left, to reach a car park after 100m on the right. Follow the road uphill from here to reach the old smaller car park from where a well-signed path climbs through the mixed woodland. As you continue to rise, you cross a track, skirt around the woodland and turn left onto a small track. Go over another forestry track, following the path across a bridge over the Moulin Burn and through the trees, before finally emerging onto the open moor via a gate.

As you cross this heather moorland, Ben Vrackie comes into view for the first

◀ Ben Vrackie

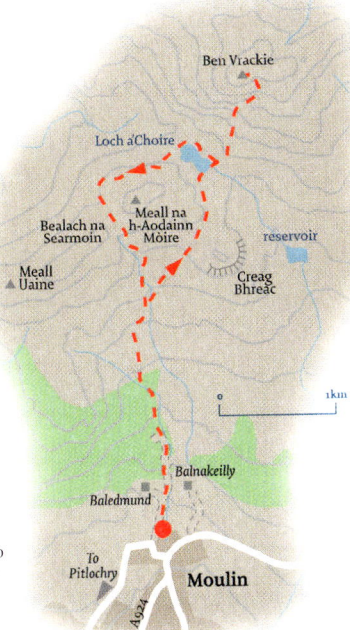

time. There is also a good outlook back to Pitlochry and across the River Tummel. Stay on the main path, ignoring a fork to the left. The branch-off is part of the Bealach Walk and can be used as the return route if you choose to make the optional extension around Loch a'Choire. Go through another gate to follow a path up a gentle incline. After rounding a corner, it starts to dip down towards the loch where, on the far side, the steep path can be seen snaking up the side of Ben Vrackie. Pass a beautifully carved wooden seat, keeping to the path as it crosses the small dam and then the outlet burn via stepping stones.

Now the hard part begins. The climb to the summit is steep but the path is good, having been recently pitched with stone to counteract the erosion caused by so many boots on this popular hill. At the top is a viewpoint indicator and, on a clear day, you can see Ben Lawers and Schiehallion, Beinn a'Ghlo and many other Cairngorms peaks from here. On a day of exceptional visibility, it is claimed that a keen eye will pick out Arthur's Seat in Edinburgh.

The easiest and quickest route of return is to retrace your steps on the main path. However, it is possible to detour around Loch a'Choire on a quieter moorland route for part of the way. To do this, go back down the steep section of path until just before the outlet for Loch a'Choire. Here, take the clear path branching off to the right and skirt around the edge of the loch. This path can be wet underfoot until it begins to climb gently through heather beyond the water. Keep on the main path, ignoring a path to the left.

As the path narrows, you get some good views towards Blair Atholl. Descend to an obvious junction, where there is a sign for Killiecrankie to the right. Turn left here for the gradual ascent to gain the lowest point between the two hills, the Bealach na Searmoin. Here, you begin to descend to rejoin the outward route. Turn right to return downhill to the start of the walk.

The River Tay ▶

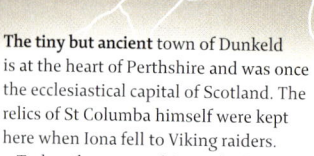

The tiny but ancient town of Dunkeld is at the heart of Perthshire and was once the ecclesiastical capital of Scotland. The relics of St Columba himself were kept here when Iona fell to Viking raiders.

Today, the pretty whitewashed cottages, attractive wynds and independent shops gather round the Cross and stretch down to the grand Telford bridge over the River Tay, whilst the ruins of the cathedral are a reminder of a more illustrious past.

Dunkeld is a great location from which to explore the region. Nearby are the famed Hermitage and Ossian's Hall, part of one of the most important designed landscapes in Scotland, visited by J M W Turner, William Wordsworth and Sir Walter Scott. It is also possible to walk from Dunkeld to Loch of the Lowes, where a telescope allows you to view the eyrie of the majestic osprey, once driven to extinction from Britain.

Just over the hills to the east is fertile Strathmore and the wilder Glen Shee, where Perthshire meets the Cairngorms. Blairgowrie is the main centre here, with its long history in the linen trade, whilst neighbouring Alyth sits on the eastern fringes of the county.

Dunkeld and Blairgowrie

1 Braan Walk and the Hermitage 30
Admire the wild waters of the Braan from the romantic follies of Ossian's Hall and Cave, and Rumbling Bridge

2 Fiddler's Path along the Tay 32
Explore the cathedral town of Dunkeld and its historic trees on this beautiful riverside circuit

3 Loch of the Lowes from the Fungarth 34
Look out for the magnificent osprey at a hidden loch above Dunkeld

4 A spell on the Tay to Birnam 36
Follow the river to an oak that sealed Macbeth's fate, returning by Birnam's Beatrix Potter Exhibition

5 Birnam Hill and Stair Bridge 38
Climb a steep wooded hill with a great outlook along the Tay, detouring to Stair Bridge for magical views

6 Cargill's Leap and the Knockie 40
Visit the site of a daring leap, a fine viewpoint and the riverside mills that brought prosperity to Blairgowrie

7 Cateran Trail to the Hill of Alyth 42
Follow the Cateran Trail and climb the twin summits above this ancient town to view the fruit farms of Strathmore

Braan Walk and the Hermitage

Distance 6.5km Time 2 hours
Terrain good paths and tracks
Map OS Explorer 379 Access bus or
train to Birnam, 1km from the start

A fine circular walk to visit the waterfalls of the Hermitage and the curious follies of Ossian's Hall and Cave.

Begin from the Hermitage car park which is signed from the A9 (charge) and begin by following the signed path beside the River Braan. Go through the underpass beneath the railway and continue along the riverbank, keeping left at a fork. Soon a picturesque bridge overlooking the dramatic Black Linn waterfall spans the river ahead. Climb up to the right to reach Ossian's Hall, which is the centrepiece of the Hermitage, a wild garden built by the son-in-law of the second Duke of Atholl in 1758.

Ossian's Hall itself is usually open and, in addition to the viewing platform, contains mirrored images from *The Poems of Ossian*. The hall was built as a viewing house for the falls and redecorated as a shrine to Ossian in 1783. The 'works' of the mythical Ossian were an epic romantic cycle of poems, published by James MacPherson in 1765, supposedly having been discovered and translated from ancient Celtic texts. The works became hugely influential, popular amongst many of Europe's elite from Sir Walter Scott to Napoleon, but today's scholars agree with Samuel Johnson's opinion that the poems were largely the work of MacPherson himself.

The romantic theme was extended to the inner room of the hall, which was originally lined with mirrors, giving visitors the impression of water cascading from all directions. William Wordsworth visited and wrote a poem describing the

Braan Walk and the Hermitage

◀ Ossian's Hall

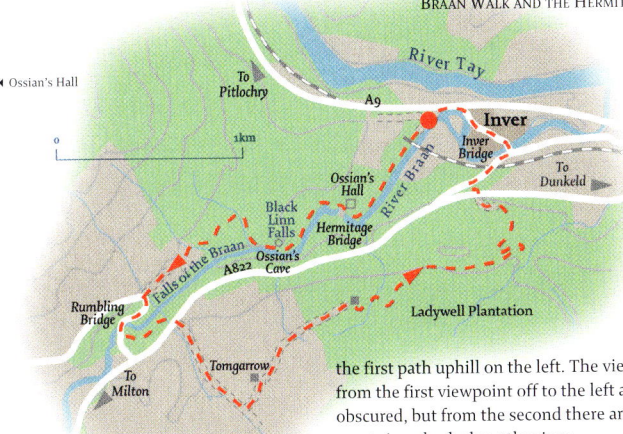

'world of wonder' of the room. In 1869, part of the hall was blown up by vandals and the building fell into decay. The National Trust for Scotland, which now owns the Hermitage, has restored it.

From the hall, turn left and proceed along the wide path for grand views of the tumbling river. Soon you reach Ossian's Cave, another folly built as part of the Hermitage. Continue straight ahead, sticking to the path nearest the river. At a crossroads, turn left and follow the green marker posts through the woods to reach a track. Turn left again to pass a pretty cottage, and go over a bridge and through a gate.

The track crosses open grazing land before coming to a road, which you follow to the left to find the tumultuous cascade beneath the Rumbling Bridge. This waterfall is a good place to spot leaping salmon in late autumn, especially after heavy rain. After crossing the bridge, take the first path uphill on the left. The views from the first viewpoint off to the left are obscured, but from the second there are great views back along the river. Eventually the path emerges from the woods at a road, which you go straight across to carry on along a track. As the track rises, turn left at a fork signposted for the Braan Walk, then curve right, past the house at Tomgarrow. Go through a gate into a woodland of birch and pine.

Just before another house, fork right and cross a small bridge and gate to enter Ladywell Plantation. When the path reaches a forestry track, turn left, noting the green markers. Keep on the main track, ignoring a branch on the right, to meet another track. A left turn here takes you to the road. Cross this to descend through the trees to reach a minor road, opposite the Inver car park. Follow the road to the right and take the next left to cross the River Braan. Head through the attractive hamlet of Inver until the road eventually becomes a footpath running parallel with the A9 to return to the entrance of the Hermitage car park.

Fiddler's Path along the Tay

Distance 10.5km **Time** 3 hours
Terrain waymarked riverside paths, minor road **Map** OS Explorer 379 **Access** buses and trains to Dunkeld/Birnam

Follow the mighty River Tay upstream from Dunkeld's bustling high street and spectacular ruined cathedral before returning on the opposite side of the water passing some remarkable trees – including the Mother Larch and Niel Gow's Oak.

Start from the Atholl Street car park at the north end of Dunkeld (charge). The waymarked path begins from the far end of the car park, signposted for the cathedral and Fiddler's Path. Follow it as it curves left around the foot of Stanley Hill, then keep right at a fork to head towards the cathedral. Turn right along the iron railings enclosing the cathedral grounds. Near the tower stands the magnificent Mother Larch – one of five European larches imported by the Duke of Atholl from Austria in 1738. The seeds of these trees went on to forest much of Perthshire with the 3rd and 4th Dukes responsible for planting around 14 million trees – the area is still known as the Big Tree County today.

At the path junction follow the Fiddler's Path left to reach the banks of the Tay, Scotland's longest river. Aim right to head upstream. At a fork the left branch is more scenic being closer to the water and passes a stone grotto, but the two routes rejoin further on. Stay on the riverbank path, ignoring a path to the right, soon walking on a surfaced, shared cyclepath with the Dunkeld House Hotel visible to the right. At the fork stay on the main cyclepath which soon runs high above the river.

After another 2km pass beneath the Jubilee Bridge which carries the

FIDDLER'S PATH ALONG THE TAY

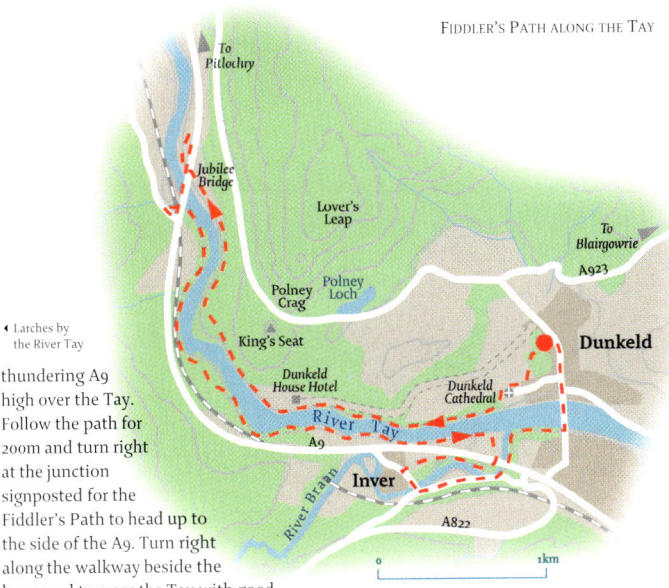

◀ Larches by the River Tay

thundering A9 high over the Tay. Follow the path for 200m and turn right at the junction signposted for the Fiddler's Path to head up to the side of the A9. Turn right along the walkway beside the busy road to cross the Tay with good views upriver towards Ben Vrackie. On the far side turn right alongside the branch road, and then right again onto a signed footpath down through the trees.

The path heads under the railway and back under the A9. Keep left at a fork to follow the riverbank, eventually climbing slightly to join a wider path. Stay on the main path, which soon returns back down to the water and then leaves the woods to follow the edge of a field.

In the 18th century a locally born man, Niel Gow, rose from humble beginnings to become Scotland's most famous fiddler. He lived at Inver and composed many tunes under the oak that now bears his name. After the path returns to the riverside you can catch a first glimpse of the Tay Bridge at Dunkeld. Turn right away from the river to reach the River Braan. The footbridge which once stood here was washed away in a flood and until it is replaced the route continues upriver under the A9. When the path forks keep right, eventually reaching the minor road in Inver. Turn left to cross Inver Bridge and keep left at the T-junction. After 500m turn left onto a path that follows the other side of the Braan back under the A9. Ignore a path off right, instead continuing by the River Braan to soon reach the River Tay once more with views to Dunkeld Cathedral over the water. Head under the Tay Bridge and up the steps on the right, then turn right to cross the bridge and return along Dunkeld's main street.

Loch of the Lowes from the Fungarth

Distance 8km **Time** 2 hours 30
Terrain paths, track and minor road
Map OS Explorer 379 **Access** Dunkeld is well served by buses and coaches; train station at nearby Birnam

This waymarked circuit explores the rolling countryside north of Dunkeld and offers the chance to watch the famous ospreys at the Loch of the Lowes. A hide (admission fee) managed by the Scottish Wildlife Trust is equipped with spotting scopes overlooking the eyrie. The route also explores Dunkeld, which can be used as an alternative start point.

The walk starts at the Cally car park, 1km north of Dunkeld on a track off the A923 to Blairgowrie. From the entrance to the car park head straight across onto the track opposite, signposted for the Loch of the Lowes. Go past the gate and after a short while take two right turns in quick succession, signposted for Drumbuie Woodlands, to dive into the trees on the right. After heading downhill, bear left at a waymarker to follow a path through fine beechwoods high above the A923.

When the path emerges at the road, cross and turn left to pick up a path on the far side. After a boardwalk, turn left up the lane towards the golf club. At the far right-hand corner of the car park, take the path signposted for the Loch of the Lowes. Bear left over a grassy area to a kissing gate and continue along the track through a wooden gate. The pleasantly wooded route leads past a cottage before swinging left and rising to join another lovely old track running across the hillside.

From this junction it is worth detouring to the Loch of the Lowes. Follow the lane left downhill to reach a minor road. Cross this and join the path on the far side, which runs through the trees just to the

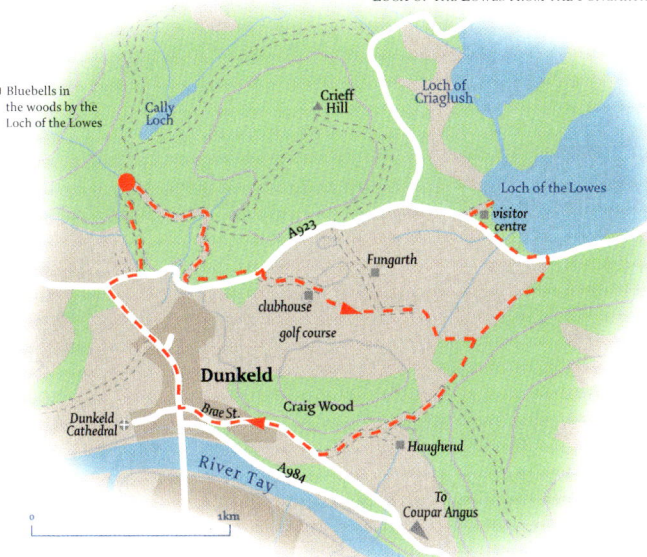

◀ Bluebells in the woods by the Loch of the Lowes

right of the road with glimpses out over the water. After a short distance, you'll come to the parking area for the Scottish Wildlife Trust reserve. The main attraction here is the nesting ospreys which can be seen between April and August. However, there is also a huge variety of birds both on the loch and around the feeders by the visitor centre. The entry fee includes the use of powerful telescopes and live CCTV footage beamed from the osprey eyrie itself. Ospreys are a real success story for this part of Perthshire. Having been persecuted and hunted to extinction in Britain, they returned to the area to nest in 1969.

Return uphill to the junction where you left the track earlier, this time carrying straight on for Dunkeld. When you meet another track, bear right and then right again at the road to pass some houses. The approach to Dunkeld is steeply downhill, with good views over the town's fine 18th-century buildings and cottages to the cathedral. Turn right along the main street.

Unless you wish to explore Dunkeld's excellent shops, cafés and pubs, simply follow the road out through the town, passing the ornate gateway to the Dunkeld House Hotel on the far side. At the T-junction with the main road, turn right towards Blairgowrie; take care as there is no pavement on this short section. The second turning on the left, beside an attractive cottage, takes you back to the Cally car park.

A spell on the Tay to Birnam

Distance 6km **Time** 1 hour 30
Terrain riverside paths and roads
Map OS Explorer 379 **Access** Dunkeld is well served by buses and coaches; train station at nearby Birnam

An easy waymarked circuit taking in the ancient Birnam Oak and a lovely stretch of the River Tay before returning through Birnam, where you can visit Birnam Arts with its art gallery, café and enchanting Beatrix Potter exhibition and garden.

The walk begins from the Tay Terrace car park in Dunkeld. Head along Tay Terrace back into the village, passing the Taybank, a renowned hub for folk music. At the main street, turn left to cross the fine Dunkeld Bridge over the Tay before turning down a flight of stone steps on the left, next to the tiny former tollhouse, and then turning right to head downstream along the riverbank.

The Tay is Scotland's longest river, beginning its journey as the River Cononish on the slopes of Ben Lui, just 32km from Oban – nearer to the west than east coast. It becomes the Tay as it flows from Loch Tay and, by the time it reaches Dunkeld, its wide waters are renowned amongst anglers for salmon-fishing. From mid-January to the end of November, you're likely to spot fishing boats as well as wader-clad fly fishermen waist-deep in water. Sometimes salmon can be seen leaping out of the water as they head upstream to spawn. It is an even more amazing sight when you consider that those same fish, having spent their early life on the river, will have since completed an epic journey to the saltwater feeding grounds of the North Sea and the Atlantic. Some may have reached the west coast of Greenland before returning, a distance of almost 10,000km as the crow flies.

A SPELL ON THE TAY TO BIRNAM

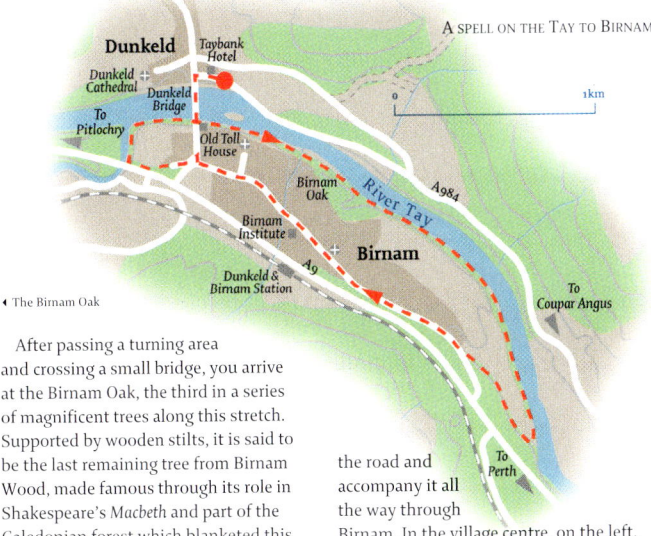

◀ The Birnam Oak

After passing a turning area and crossing a small bridge, you arrive at the Birnam Oak, the third in a series of magnificent trees along this stretch. Supported by wooden stilts, it is said to be the last remaining tree from Birnam Wood, made famous through its role in Shakespeare's *Macbeth* and part of the Caledonian forest which blanketed this area 1000 years ago. In the play, the three witches promised that:

Macbeth shall never vanquish'd be until
Great Birnam wood to high Dunsinane hill
Shall come against him.

As this was some distance away, Macbeth believed his throne to be secure, but his enemies attacked after approaching Dunsinane camouflaged in branches from the wood, and Macbeth was overthrown.

Keep following the main path beyond the oak, ignoring the turning into Birnam. Further on, some spectacular large beech trees line the riverside. At a fishing jetty and hut, make a right turn onto a track which leads you away from the water to meet a road. Cross this to go through the kissing gate opposite and another one beyond, where you now turn right onto the road and accompany it all the way through Birnam. In the village centre, on the left, you'll see the Birnam Institute, now known as Birnam Arts – home to an excellent café and live performances as well as a gallery and the Beatrix Potter Exhibition. A small public garden contains bronze sculptures of Potter's characters: the artist and writer spent much time in this area as a young woman and a letter she wrote here led to the creation of *The Tale of Peter Rabbit*.

At the junction after the school, go straight across the main road and follow the minor road opposite. The road soon becomes a surfaced path which leads you to the River Braan. Turn right to shadow the Braan to the point where it shortly joins the River Tay, with a splendid view across the water to the cathedral. At Dunkeld Bridge, return up the steps by the tollhouse and cross the bridge to the start.

5 DUNKELD AND BLAIRGOWRIE

Birnam Hill and Stair Bridge

Distance 6km **Time** 2 hours 30
Terrain rough paths, some boggy ground, very steep descent **Map** OS Explorer 379
Access footpath from train station in Birnam or bus to Birnam Quarry

This more strenuous circuit rewards with an enchanting outlook over Dunkeld and the surrounding countryside. The ascent to the viewpoint is long and reasonably gentle, but the descent is very steep.

The walk starts at the Birnam Quarry lay-by just off the A9 on the B867, 1km south of Birnam. It is possible to reach this walk on foot from the train station at Birnam by passing under the railway and turning left via the red marker signs, joining the route at the bottom of the descent from Birnam Hill.

From the parking area, walk under the railway and follow the track for a very short distance, looking out for a signed turning on the left. Keep to the path as it climbs steadily through mixed woodland. Further on, there are views over the railway line as the path accompanies a fence and then a wall uphill, before levelling off as it starts to curve around the slopes to the right. At a junction, the route continues to the right but you can make a short detour to Stair Bridge by going straight on. This ancient stone bridge gives magical views down the glen towards Rohallion Lodge, a fairytale turreted castle set by a loch and forest. Return to the main route and continue around the flank of Birnam Hill.

The path soon leaves the trees and

Birnam Hill and Stair Bridge

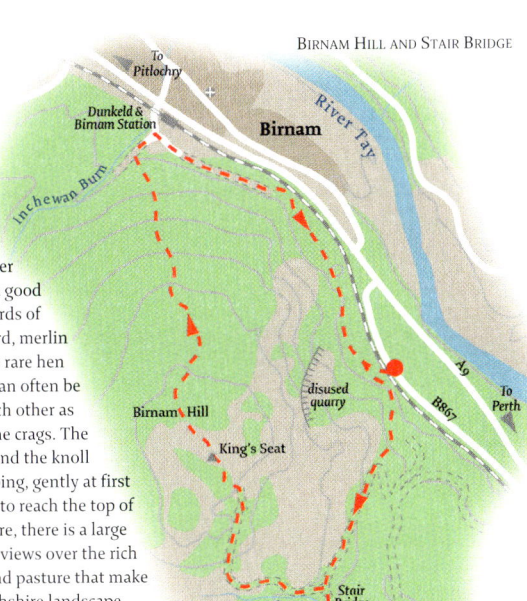

◄ On Birnam Hill

crosses open heather moorland. This is a good area for spotting birds of prey such as buzzard, merlin and sometimes the rare hen harrier. The birds can often be heard calling to each other as they circle above the crags. The path contours around the knoll ahead before climbing, gently at first and then up steps, to reach the top of the King's Seat. Here, there is a large cairn and fantastic views over the rich green woodland and pasture that make up this classic Perthshire landscape.

From the top, a distinct path drops downhill. There are a couple of rocky sections near the top which require care, and then a boggy area, before good views over Dunkeld and Birnam are revealed from a rocky crag. The path now begins a steep descent through woods. Further down, you may be grateful to find a seat as the path is unrelentingly steep and can be slippery after rain. Keep an eye out for mountain bikers as they tear down this section. At the bottom, turn right onto a wide path which soon turns into a track and then a road which passes between houses. Keep right at any junctions.

Beyond the houses, you'll see a sign marking the track ahead as private. This route turns left just before the sign to access a marked path which meanders through the woods, crossing a small wooden bridge at one point. This part of the walk can be noisy at times, as it runs close to the busy A9. Keep following the path until it emerges onto a track. The route goes straight across this to continue on a pathway: if, however, it appears to be too boggy, an alternative is to simply walk down the track, as the path rejoins it later.

Assuming you have taken the path, turn right when you re-emerge on the track for a gentle descent which passes back under the railway to the start of the walk.

Cargill's Leap and the Knockie

Distance 6km **Time** 2 hours
Terrain waymarked paths, tracks and minor roads **Map** OS Explorer 381
Access Blairgowrie is well served by buses from Perth and Dundee

This varied circuit follows the River Ericht upstream, with waterfalls, woodland and old mills along the way. The return is over the Knockie, a viewpoint which looks out over Blairgowrie to the Sidlaw Hills.

Blairgowrie owes much of its past prosperity to the power of the River Ericht, explored on this walk. The town was built around the textile industry which harnessed the fast-flowing water to run mills spinning flax, some weaving it into linen and others processing jute.

This walk starts at the William MacPherson Park car park on the riverside near the centre of town, where you'll find an information board and picnic tables. To access it on foot, go down the steps next to the bridge, passing the steel fish sculpture. From the car park, take the path that heads upstream. After a fairly short distance, the path goes left up a flight of wooden steps to reach an upper track. Turn right along this, now high above the river.

On the right, a flight of wooden steps down to a viewing platform makes a good detour. The path soon rejoins the main track; continue along it before branching off on the right to a second viewing platform overlooking a series of cataracts in the river below. This is Cargill's Leap, where Donald Cargill, a local minster and covenanter, escaped pursuing troops by leaping the falls. He was eventually captured and, after uttering his final words 'Death to the believer is just like putting off a worn suit of clothes, and putting on a new suit', he was executed in July 1681.

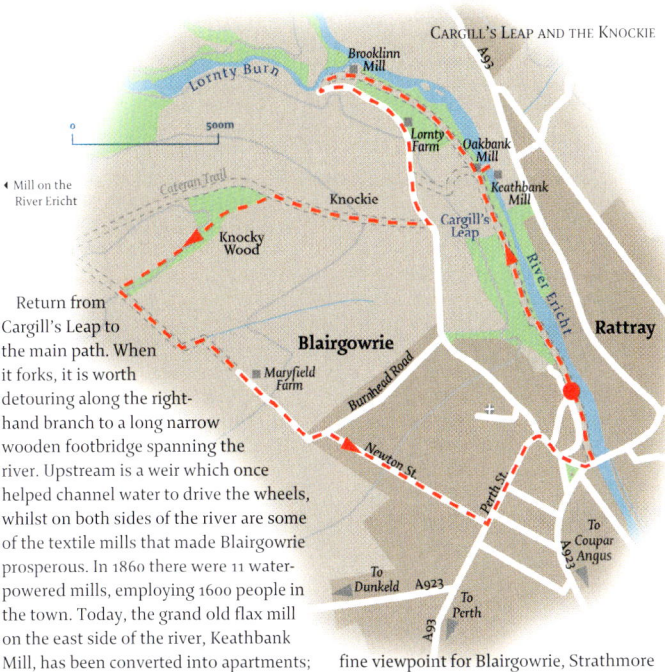

◀ Mill on the River Ericht

Return from Cargill's Leap to the main path. When it forks, it is worth detouring along the right-hand branch to a long narrow wooden footbridge spanning the river. Upstream is a weir which once helped channel water to drive the wheels, whilst on both sides of the river are some of the textile mills that made Blairgowrie prosperous. In 1860 there were 11 water-powered mills, employing 1600 people in the town. Today, the grand old flax mill on the east side of the river, Keathbank Mill, has been converted into apartments; the smaller one on the near side is Oakbank Mill. Do not cross the river; instead return to the track running upstream. Pass some old millworkers' cottages and then Brooklinn Mill, now a private home. At the minor road, turn left for a gentle climb past Lornty Farm. After another 400m, turn right onto a tarmac lane (signposted Cateran Trail) and climb through rich mixed farmland.

At the edge of a wood, a small waymarker indicates where to bear left to follow a narrow winding path through the trees. Eventually this emerges at benches and a view indicator. This is the Knockie, a fine viewpoint for Blairgowrie, Strathmore and the Sidlaw Hills.

Turn left to take the grassy lane which winds down the hill, passing first some newer houses and then an old farmhouse, before swinging left to reach the end of Burnhead Road. Turn right onto Newton Street here, going straight through several crossroads and all the way down to Perth Street. Turn left along this, keeping with it as it bends right, to reach the top of the Wellmeadow. Continue along the road until you reach the bridge over the River Ericht – do not cross but instead turn left on the riverside path, passing a sculpture to return to the start.

Cateran Trail to the Hill of Alyth

Distance 6.5km **Time** 2 hours 30
Terrain minor road, track and moorland path, boggy and indistinct in places; a steep climb **Map** OS Explorer 381
Access bus to Alyth from Blairgowrie, Perth and Dundee

Two hills for just one climb is the bargain claim of this circuit. Starting in Alyth, the route climbs steeply, but is rewarded by fantastic views of the Sidlaw Hills to the south and the Cairngorms to the north.

Alyth is a fine little town with a history stretching back to the 11th century. The walk begins from the parking area in the centre, crossing the burn and turning left to follow the east bank past the Alyth Hotel. At the far end is a packhorse bridge, thought to date from 1500. Continue along Toutie Street and up the steep rise before turning right into Hill Street at the top. Bear left into Loyal Road, following the green signs for the 102km Cateran Trail, which mostly follows old drovers' routes through the countryside around Blairgowrie. It is named after the gangs of cattle thieves known as caterans who flourished in this part of the Highlands from the middle ages until well into the 17th century.

After passing the entrance to the Lands of Loyal Hotel on the right, continue ahead through a metal gate and follow the track for a short steep climb with ever-improving views back over Strathmore and the Sidlaw Hills.

The gradient eases a little before steepening for a final push to the crest of the hill. After reaching the three gates, take the right-hand one and make the short detour climb to the top of the Hill of Loyal. Cross the boggy burn and after 50m diverge from the fence and head northeast through the trees, following rough ATV tracks and forking left to aim for the highest ground. There is a boggy stretch

CATERAN TRAIL TO THE HILL OF ALYTH

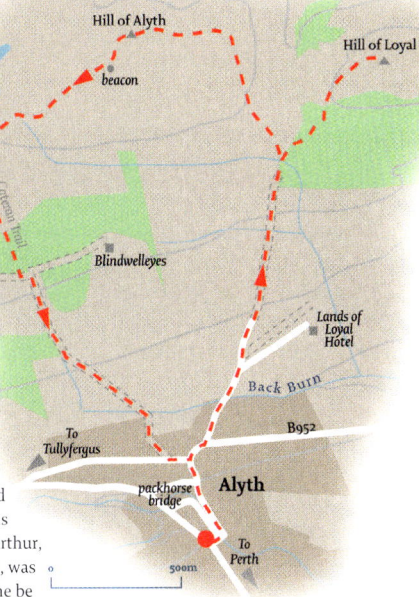

◀ Barry Hill Fort from the Hill of Loyal

before the gorse gives way to heather and grass. At the summit, it is worth dropping slightly to the east, aiming for the right edge of some pine trees, and going along as far as the fence for a view over the rings of the fort on neighbouring Barry Hill.

Legend suggests that this fort may have been the castle where the Pictish King Mordred took Queen Guinevere prisoner following the defeat of her husband King Arthur. Scottish tradition states that Guinevere did not find her captor as repugnant as might be thought and that King Arthur, on learning of his wife's infidelity, was so enraged that he ordered that she be torn to pieces by wild horses; she is supposedly buried nearby. Archaeologists have since dismissed Barry Hill's place in history by deciding the fort is not ancient enough to have played this part in the tale.

Return to the gate and this time go right through a pedestrian gate. Ignore the sign for the Cateran Trail and take the grassy path rising diagonally uphill. Where the path forks, keep right to climb through gorse. Keep along it to eventually reach the trig point at the top of the Hill of Alyth. There's a good view of the Sidlaw Hills, while in the opposite direction you'll see the hills beyond Glen Isla. On a clear day, the view extends all the way to Ben Lawers and, slightly nearer, Schiehallion.

From here follow the path as it turns left, then back right. The next section is hard to follow; the objective is Alyth Millennium Beacon which lies around 400m to the southwest but remains out of sight until you reach it. Take the middle path of three up a bank and then continue along this path to pass the beacon. The path soon joins the Cateran Trail which leads down towards Alyth. After following fences, follow the old drove road past farm buildings to meet the High Street, then turn right down Toutie Street to return to the start of the walk.

Loch Tay is the sixth largest loch in Scotland, stretching 22km from Killin, just over the border in Stirlingshire to the west, to the 18th-century planned village of Kenmore with its whitewashed cottages and elegant bridge to the east. The loch is scattered with tiny man-made islands, or crannogs, defensive dwellings dating back to the Iron Age.

To the north of Loch Tay is the mighty Ben Lawers mountain range, concealing behind it Glen Lyon, which was described by Sir Walter Scott as the 'longest, loneliest and loveliest glen in Scotland'. Today, it is still a peaceful retreat well worth venturing off the beaten track for.

The largest settlement in this area is further east at Aberfeldy, a handsome stone-built town tightly clustered around its central square. Its showpiece is the Birks, an enchanting wooded ravine whose waterfalls are celebrated in song by Robert Burns. This whole area also forms part of the historic district of Breadalbane, meaning High Country – you'll see frequent references to this locally.

Highland cow, Glen Lyon ▸

Killin, Kenmore and Aberfeldy

1. **The Birks of Aberfeldy** 46
Admire the dizzying spectacle of the Moness gorge on this picturesque loop

2. **Black Rock from Kenmore** 48
Enjoy one of the most outstanding views over Loch Tay on Drummond Hill

3. **Kenmore Hill above Loch Tay** 50
Watch for rare black grouse on this hill tour, returning by the Queen's Drive

4. **Falls of Acharn and the Hermit's Cave** 52
Let the splendour of the falls above the pretty village of Acharn be revealed through a dramatic framing device

5. **Glen Lyon and Bridge of Balgie** 54
Make a meal of the 'longest, loneliest and loveliest glen' in Scotland with a stop-off at a charming tearoom

6. **Edramucky Trail** 56
Take the high road to hunt for Ben Lawers' renowned wildflowers

7. **Killin and Loch Tay** 58
Follow the old railway line to the shores of mighty Loch Tay and return by the River Lochay

8. **Fingal's Stone and Sron a'Chlachain** 60
Climb high above Killin to see the whole of Loch Tay and the village unfold in miniature below

9. **Falls of Dochart to Acharn Woods** 62
Weave through a wooded wildlife haven by Killin against the backdrop of the knobbly Tarmachan Ridge

The Birks of Aberfeldy

Distance 3.5km **Time** 1 hour 30
Terrain narrow paths, steps and steep sections **Map** OS Explorer 379
Access Aberfeldy is well served by buses

This very popular short walk heads up the Moness gorge to visit the series of waterfalls immortalised in the Burns ballad 'The Birks of Aberfeldy'. The birch, oak, ash and elms which cling to the gorge are spectacular in the autumn.

The walk begins from the Birks car park, which is accessed by a signed path from the main square in Aberfeldy if setting out on foot. From the upper car park, take the obvious trail, bearing left to cross the large bridge over the foaming Moness Burn. This lower part of the Birks is predominantly a beechwood; it becomes more varied as the soil quality changes further up.

Whilst there were great forests in this area when man first arrived about 5000 years ago, the woods that are here today were planted much later. The original Caledonian forest was cleared for timber and to make space for growing crops. In fact, deforestation in Scotland was so complete that when Dr Johnson toured the country in 1773 he commented that 'a tree in Scotland is as rare as a horse in Venice'. Towards the end of the 18th century, landowners began to replant as the economic value of timber increased and trees became fashionable as part of a 'scenic' landscape. Records show that the gorge, then called the Den of Moness, was planted in the late 1780s. Some of the trees that cling to the steep sides are likely to be relics of the original forest, however, as their inaccessibility means that they were unlikely to have been cut down or grazed.

The walk follows the clear path beside the burn, passing several small waterfalls. (The walking trail, the Rob Roy Way, also shares this trail as the approach to

THE BIRKS OF ABERFELDY

◀ Moness Burn

Aberfeldy.) As it narrows into the gorge, the path has a handrail. Cross a bridge over a feeder burn with attractive falls on the left. Just beyond is a natural shelf in the rocks known as Burns' Seat. It was here that Robert Burns is said to have taken a rest when he visited in 1787. The visit inspired his ballad 'The Birks of Aberfeldy' and, following the rise in popularity of the den (meaning 'wooded glen' in Scots), the Moness Estate built a path and opened it up to the public. As you gain height, the large beech trees are left behind to be replaced by ash, wych elm, hazel and willow in the wetter spots. These damp conditions are also perfect for mosses: there are at least 10 different species just around Burns' Seat alone.

The climb continues up several flights of stone steps and switchbacks, with views over a series of cascades, before following the wooden walkway up the gorge. At the end of this, the path forks. Detour straight ahead to reach a viewpoint for the Middle Falls, where the Moness Burn flows through a ravine. Afterwards, return to the path, where a brief clearing soon gives a good view of the dramatic Upper Moness Falls. This landscape, with its steep-sided U-shaped valleys, was carved by retreating glaciers during the last ice age 10,000 years ago. The glaciers left steep drops from hanging valleys like the one the waterfall tumbles over today. Next, the path crosses the footbridge over the Upper Falls. If you have a head for heights, this is a spot to appreciate the power of the water as tree trunks, swept down in earlier spates, lie smashed on the gorge floor far below.

The path now bears right to return down the other side of the gorge. The woodland here is mostly birches, or 'birks' in Scots. Together with rowan and willow, these trees can tolerate poor soil and windy conditions. The descent gives plenty of good tree-framed views and is easy to follow back to the car park.

Black Rock from Kenmore

Distance 7km **Time** 2 hours
Terrain waymarked tracks, paths
Map OS Explorer 379 **Access** bus to
Kenmore from Aberfeldy and Killin

Combine two waymarked walks on Drummond Hill to visit the stunning Black Rock viewpoint over Loch Tay and glimpse huge Taymouth Castle. This hill is also home to the rare capercaillie.

After the First World War, Drummond Hill was one of the first sites to be bought by the new Forestry Commission which was set up to replant the forestry felled for timber as part of the war effort. Prior to this, the hill had been used for forestry experiments and was chosen as the reintroduction site for the capercaillie in 1837, the bird having previously been hunted to extinction in Britain. Thanks to the extensive covering of Scots pine, the capercaillie has continued to survive on Drummond Hill, although the bird is still endangered and, given its shy nature, rarely seen. You stand a better chance of hearing one: the distinctive clip-clop sound gives it its name, meaning 'Horse of the Woods' in Gaelic.

Start from the signposted Forestry and Land Scotland car park about 1km from Kenmore on the minor road turning right off the A827 just north of Kenmore Bridge. A wide track leads from the information boards into the forest; follow the blue and red waymarker to keep straight ahead when a path peels off to the right. The mixed woods are left behind on the ascent as the larches, spruces and Douglas Firs favoured by commercial forestry take over. After a sharp right-hand bend, the track steepens. At an angled crossroads, a left turn and then another leads out onto the rocky outcrop known as Black Rock. The view over Loch Tay and Kenmore is

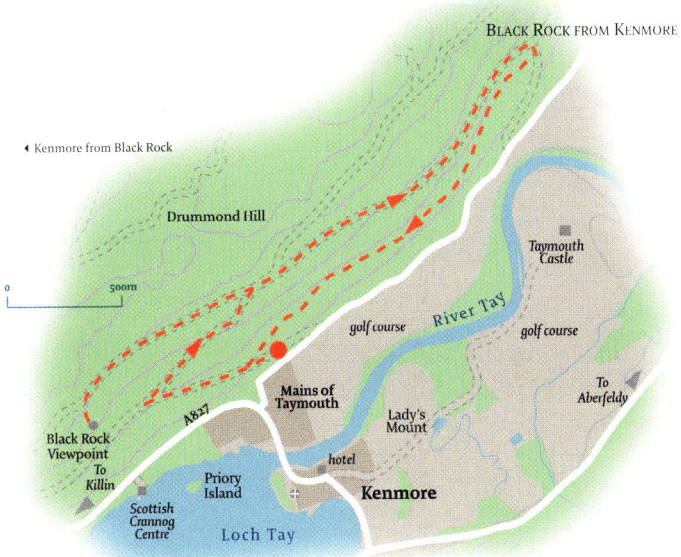

◀ Kenmore from Black Rock

BLACK ROCK FROM KENMORE

spectacular. A reconstructed Iron Age crannog, with its pointy thatched roof, perched high above the water on wooden stilts lies just offshore below, whilst further out is Priory Island, burial place of the 13th-century Queen Sybilla of Scotland. The viewpoint is bounded by a stone wall, built in the style of the walls around the designed landscape of Taymouth Castle.

Return to the angled crossroads, this time observing the red marker post to simply continue ahead, downhill. There are glimpses of the massive bulk of Taymouth Castle through the trees.

Built by the Campbells of Breadalbane, the enormous baronial pile is testament to the wealth of their landowning estates which stretched from Aberfeldy all the way to the west coast. The present building dates largely from the 19th century but stands on the site of the ancient Balloch Castle, built in 1550 for Sir Colin Campbell of Glenorchy. His son, known as Black Duncan, was responsible for the original planting of Drummond Hill in the early 17th century.

A red marker post indicates where to turn right along a sometimes muddy path as it dives back through very densely planted forestry. The trees eventually thin out and, as the path slopes gently uphill, native trees replace the pines with good opportunities for wildlife watching. The undulating path passes above the car park to eventually join the track followed early in the walk. Turn left along this to return to the start.

Kenmore Hill above Loch Tay

Distance 5km **Time** 2 hours
Terrain waymarked, rough hill paths
Map OS Explorer 379 **Access** bus from Aberfeldy and Killin to Kenmore, 1.5km north of the start (steep climb)

This waymarked circuit has superb views over Loch Tay and the mountains beyond.

The walk starts from the small car park (signposted Woodland Walks), just a short way south of Kenmore on the slightly hair-raising Amulree road. It is the longest of the waymarked trails here and has red marker posts. From the information board, branch right uphill. As the path winds up through the young trees, it gives great views back to Strath Tay and the imposing block of Taymouth Castle.

After crossing a small burn, you'll come to a fork, where you bear right to cross wooden boards to a stile. Don't cross the stile; instead keep left towards a gate, but don't pass through this either. The red waymarkers lead uphill through an area where several grand old Scots pines are all that remain of the ancient Caledonian forest of mixed pine and broadleaf species that once blanketed the area. Tree-felling began in the Iron Age and, more recently, grazing animals have made regeneration impossible. However, the landowner, Bolfracks Estate, has been working with the Forestry Commission and the local Countryside Trust to recreate a natural woodland on Kenmore Hill, including the planting of native trees and partial fencing to prevent overgrazing.

The area is home to the black grouse, an endangered species. If up and about early, you may be lucky enough to witness their very distinctive courtship ritual, or lek, which usually takes place at daybreak during spring. The males display their fan-shaped black tail feathers to expose the white feathers underneath whilst making a distinctive bubbling call. This exhibition

KENMORE HILL ABOVE LOCH TAY

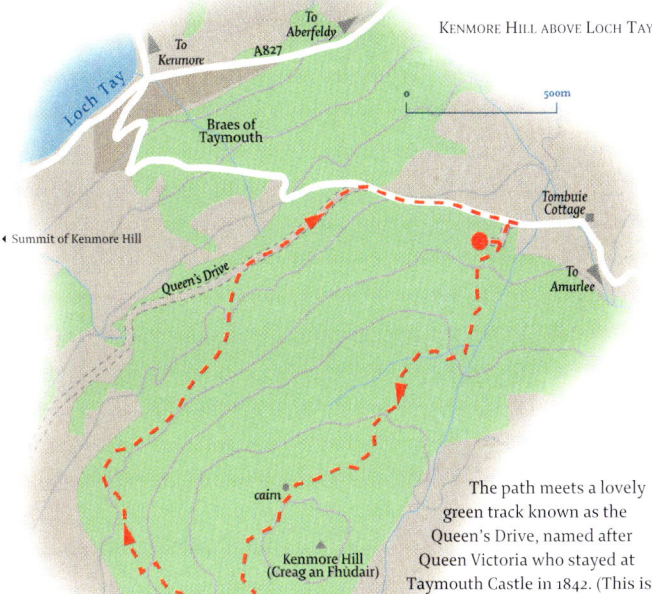

attracts the smaller brown hens who then choose their mate.

The path eventually arrives at a massive cairn near the summit. The highest point is away from the trail over to the left, but this cairn is by far the best viewpoint. Below, almost half the length of Loch Tay can be seen, backed by the towering summits of the Ben Lawers range. Further to the right is the Carn Mairg group of four Munros, while almost directly behind Kenmore is the cone of Schiehallion. From the cairn, carry on along the path to soon cross a stile over a deer fence. Turn left alongside the fence before curving to the right and dropping down through densely planted forestry.

The path meets a lovely green track known as the Queen's Drive, named after Queen Victoria who stayed at Taymouth Castle in 1842. (This is also part of the Rob Roy Way.) Turn right for great views over the foot of Loch Tay and Kenmore. From here, the importance of Kenmore's waterside location can be appreciated. Situated on a small peninsula where the River Tay drains the loch, it was created as a model village in the 1760s by the 3rd Earl of Breadalbane, replacing an earlier settlement gathered around a ford. The village celebrates the start of the salmon-fishing season every January with a celebrity-stacked party and, during the summer months, it plays host to loch fishermen and watersports enthusiasts. The track finally reaches a large gate and the minor road just beyond. Turn right to climb up the road, reaching the entrance to the car park after about 500m.

Falls of Acharn and the Hermit's Cave

Distance 5.5km **Time** 2 hours
Terrain clear paths and tracks, steep climb
Map OS Explorer OL48 **Access** no public transport to the start; bus from Aberfeldy and Killin to Kenmore, 2km from the start

This beautiful walk visits the Falls of Acharn, set in a steep wooded ravine, and climbs uphill to an ancient stone circle with spectacular views. Popular with travellers since Victorian times, the falls are approached through a 'Hermit's Cave', which adds to the drama and splendour of the setting.

The village of Acharn was built early in the 19th century to house workers from the neighbouring estates. There is space to park on the west side of the Acharn Burn along the left side of a signposted track for the Falls of Acharn, opposite a beautiful old stone cottage. Follow the sign to walk up the track past the attractive gardens: here, you are on the Rob Roy Way, a long-distance walking route linking Drymen, just east of Loch Lomond, to Pitlochry.

A steep climb gives increasingly good views back across Loch Tay to the peaks of Ben Lawers and its nearer neighbour, Meall Greigh. After about 500m, a path peels off to the left and immediately plunges into the entrance to the Hermit's Cave. This artificial, stone-built cave was constructed in the 1760s by the 3rd Earl of Breadalbane to give the most dramatic approach to the falls by concealing them from view until the last moment. A popular tourist attraction since Victorian times, its visitors have included Robert Burns, William Wordsworth and his sister Dorothy.

The cave is dark inside, but there is

FALLS OF ACHARN AND THE HERMIT'S CAVE

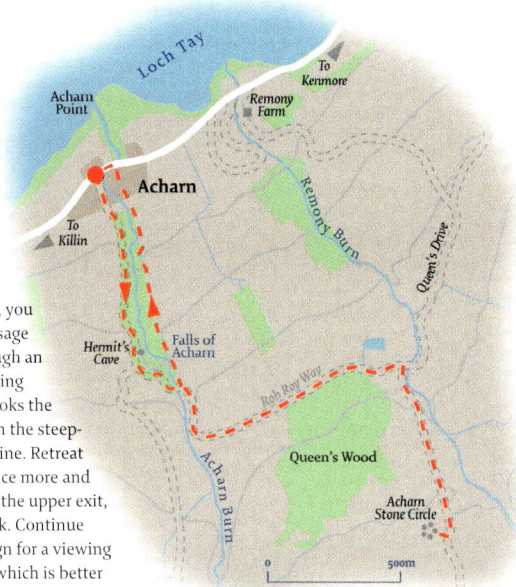

◀ Falls of Acharn

enough light to find your way. In a while, you turn left along a passage that opens out through an archway onto a viewing balcony. This overlooks the highest of the falls in the steep-sided beech-clad ravine. Retreat into the darkness once more and turn left to leave via the upper exit, returning to the track. Continue uphill, ignoring a sign for a viewing platform to the left which is better reached on the walk back down from the other side of the gorge.

A little higher up, the track crosses a stone bridge above the ravine. Before returning down the far side, go uphill to visit the stone circle. Go through the gate and follow the main track keeping left of the burn, soon passing below Queen's Wood. Beyond the wood, turn right at a junction to follow a grassy track over grazing land. After 500m, go through a gate in a stone wall to reach the stone circle. There are four standing stones and two fallen ones occupying a fantastic position overlooking the loch and mountains of the Ben Lawers range.

Head all the way back to the stone bridge; don't cross but keep right to walk down the side of the gorge. Don't miss the detour onto the wooden viewing platforms suspended over the burn to the left. Built by the army in 1989, these give views of the attractive upper falls as well as the weirdly sculpted rocks and potholes of the riverbed.

Return to the main path to continue the descent through fine mature woodland back down to the road. Turn left to return across the bridge to Acharn.

Glen Lyon and Bridge of Balgie

Distance 4.5km **Time** 1 hour 30
Terrain woodland path across steep slopes, minor road **Map** OS Explorer OL48
Access no public transport to the start

Glen Lyon is renowned for its great beauty, described by Sir Walter Scott as the 'longest, loneliest and loveliest glen in Scotland'. This walk explores the mid section of the glen, with fine views as it climbs through the Ben Meggernie Birchwood before returning past the excellent Glenlyon Tearoom.

Glen Lyon is a remote and very long glen, stretching for 55km from Loch Lyon at the western end to Fortingall, with its chocolate-box thatched houses and the remains of a famous 5000-year-old yew tree, which is thought to be the oldest living thing in Europe. Fortingall also claims to have been the birthplace of Pontius Pilate, supposedly the illegitimate son of a Roman officer who was sent as an envoy by Caesar Augustus some time around 50AD to establish diplomatic relations with important local chieftans.

The walk starts from the car park and public toilets at Innerwick. It is worth crossing the bridge over the Allt a'Mhuic to visit the war memorial and picturesque Innerwick Church. A broad path leads into the forestry from the car park, following red and blue waymarkers. At a junction follow the red waymarkers to the right. (The blue route is the return path from the tearoom.) The path soon takes you into beautiful natural birchwoods and heads up a series of steps. (Ignore a black waymarked trail on the right.)

The path continues to rise to a point where there is a seat with a good view over the floor of the glen. Traditionally, Glen

Glen Lyon and Bridge of Balgie

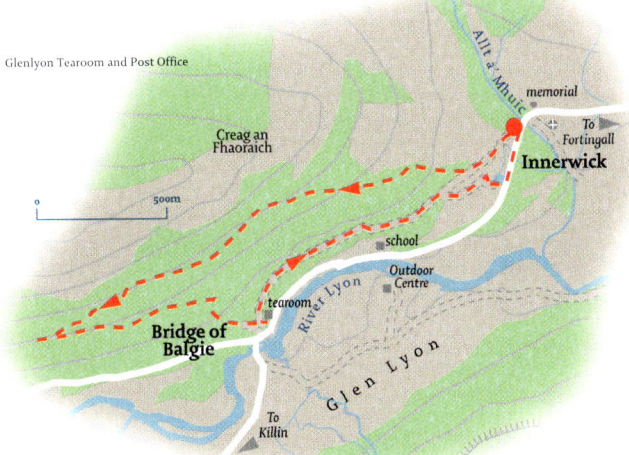

◀ Glenlyon Tearoom and Post Office

Lyon was home to the Campbells, infamous government supporters and perpetrators of the Glencoe massacre, and the MacGregors, themselves known for being a lawless, landless and outlawed clan. The fertile land in Glen Lyon was the object of cattle-rustling raids by rival clans. In the winter before the Glencoe massacre, a raid by the MacDonalds left the Campbells reliant for food on the mercies of their neighbour, Campbell of Breadalbane, the main instigator of the massacre. 'Mad' Colin Campbell, who built nearby Meggernie Castle in 1585, caught and hung 30 MacDonalds during one of the raids. The castle is a little way up the glen, but it is not open to the public.

The path now gently descends to meet another junction. The left turn provides a direct shortcut to Bridge of Balgie, but to carry on along the main route continue straight ahead following the red waymarkers to reach a viewpoint.

There is a seat at the viewpoint – a good vantage point for the mountains enclosing the upper glen. As the path drops once again, the small collection of buildings at Bridge of Balgie and the beautiful white towerhouse beside it come into view. Keep left at a junction (still following the red waymarkers) and at the next junction the return route is to the left. Carrying on downhill, however, will take you to the Glenlyon Tearoom.

To return to the start, turn back up the hill and go right, following the blue waymarkers. Keep straight on when another path joins and at a fork bear right downhill, passing a lochan before reaching the road. Go left to return to the car park.

Edramucky Trail

Distance 2km **Time** 1 hour
Terrain waymarked path, rocky steps, short steep section **Map** OS Explorer OL48
Access no public transport to the start; nearest bus service is to Killin, 10km away

This short nature trail begins from the high road between Loch Tay and Glen Lyon, giving easy access to the mid-level slopes of Ben Lawers, home to the most celebrated arctic-alpine flora in Britain and popular with Munro-baggers. Despite the ease of access, this walk is high up and exposed – so check the weather forecast and go prepared.

The walk starts from the Ben Lawers car park (charge) up the minor road to Glen Lyon, off the A827 on the north side of Loch Tay: this steep road is not always kept clear of snow and ice, and is sometimes impassable in winter. Ben Lawers is an important ecological site, its lime-rich soils supporting the rarest collection of mountain plants in Britain. Designated a National Nature Reserve, it is jointly managed by the National Trust for Scotland and NatureScot. The nature trail explores a previously fenced area where the plants have been protected from the effects of grazing sheep and deer. Some

plants and trees have been reintroduced but most are naturally regenerating.

To begin, head through the walled information area and along the path and through a gateway. Cross the road and continue on the path on the far side. Soon after, turn right to follow the smaller designated Edramucky Trail and cross the footbridge over the burn. The main path (which you return along) is the route to Ben Lawers, often busy with hikers aiming for the summit, passing over the intermediate Munro peak of Beinn Ghlas. Despite its altitude of 1214m, Ben Lawers is relatively easy by hillwalking standards and thus very popular. The National Trust for Scotland has repaired the worst of the resulting erosion through path building and encouraging people to stick to the main routes.

As the nature trail heads up the far side of the Edramucky Burn, look out for the wildflowers – many of them spring flowering – including several varieties of saxifrage. Others, such as the bristle sedge, which can only be found in Britain on Ben Lawers, are harder to spot. The path crosses the attractive stony bed of the burn to the left bank before returning to the right on stepping stones.

On this gradual ascent, the views of Loch Tay eventually unfold far below with a stunning perspective of the surrounding peaks too. The hill to the left is Meall Corranaich with Beinn Ghlas to its right: this conceals Ben Lawers from this side and is often mistaken for it. Looking back across the road is the rocky summit of Meall nan Tarmachan.

Further up, you meet the main Ben Lawers path once more, where you turn left and shortly cross the burn. This well-maintained path gives an easy descent towards the car park, rejoining the outward route to deliver you back to the start.

◀ On the Edramucky Trail

Killin and Loch Tay

Distance 3km **Time** 1 hour **Terrain** clear, flat paths **Map** OS Explorer OL48 **Access** buses to Killin from Crianlarich, Lochearnhead and Callander

Explore the shore of Loch Tay on this low-level circuit from Killin. The walk follows the line of the old railway to access the head of the loch for great views across the water and some beautiful places to picnic.

Start from the car park on the east side of Killin. To reach it from the village centre, take the turning opposite Killin Outdoor Centre (signed for toilets, parking and the old railway line) to pass St Fillans Church. From the car park, join the old railway line by going through the gate next to the toilets and turning left. This was a branch line that connected the main Callander to Oban route with Killin and Loch Tay before it closed in 1939. On the shore of the loch was a pier, where a steamer service could be boarded for the onward journey to Kenmore.

A handsome metal viaduct takes you over the River Lochay, where you can often observe canoeists on the water below. The old railway line now takes you into pleasant woodland and runs parallel to a minor road before reaching a gate after 500m which gives access to the loch.

Loch Tay is Scotland's sixth largest loch at 24km long and over 150m deep. The shores were once much more populated, but the Highland Clearances and changing economic conditions forced many to move away. During the Iron Age, there were a number of crannogs, dwellings built on stilts or artificial islands, out in the water. The remains of

◂ Loch Tay

one crannog site can just about be made out near the shore on the left. Now overgrown with trees and shrubs, it would have been part of a thriving community 5000 years ago. There is a reconstructed crannog at the Scottish Crannog Centre near Kenmore at the opposite end of the loch, where you can learn more about these fascinating structures.

Cross the head of the loch passing a number of sandy stretches. Keep following the path as it curves along the shoreline to the mouth of two rivers, the Lochay and the Dochart. Stay on the path as it heads along the banks of the River Lochay, over boardwalks in places; it can be muddy and prone to flooding. Canoeing and fishing are popular pastimes on this section. As it shadows the wide river, the path passes through a small metal gate and crosses a field before eventually returning to the old railway track at a metal gate. Turn left and cross back over the bridge to retrace your steps to the start.

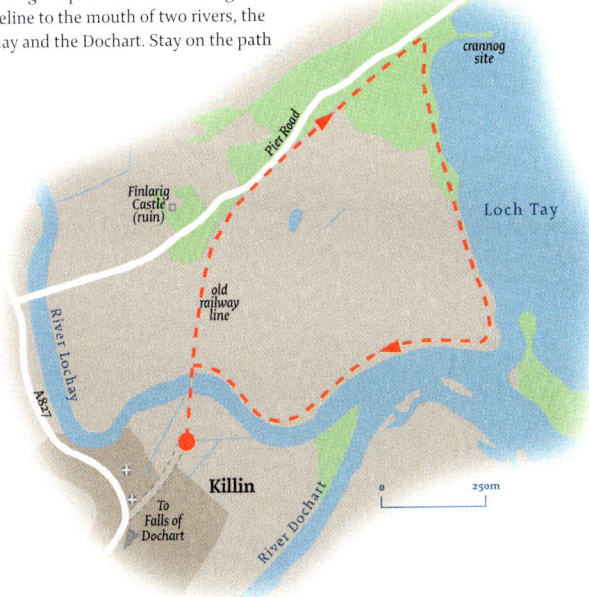

Fingal's Stone and Sron a'Chlachain

Distance 4km **Time** 2 hours
Terrain very steep path, can be slippery when wet **Map** OS Explorer OL48
Access buses to Killin from Crianlarich, Lochearnhead and Callander

This steep ascent of the hill overlooking Killin offers fabulous views down Loch Tay. The path passes through an oakwood and onto open moorland on a rewarding but strenuous climb.

Begin the walk from Breadalbane Park in the centre of Killin. There is parking next to the McLaren Hall towards the north end of the village. From here, the path leads through the park (keep the play area to your left) towards the far left corner.

Before heading through the gate you can detour to Fingal's Stone which, according to legend, is the burial place of the mythical Celtic giant who also gave his name to the cave on Staffa and the causeway in Northern Ireland. The story goes that he was challenged by his love rival Taileachd to take a giant leap backwards from an island on nearby Loch Iubhair to the shore. Fingal failed to reach land and, as he fell into the water, Taileachd seized his moment and hacked off the giant's head. Fingal's body was washed downstream and found by his followers at the Falls of Dochart, where they buried it. Taileachd fled northwards, still in possession of Fingal's head, but

Fingal's Stone and Sron a'Chlachain

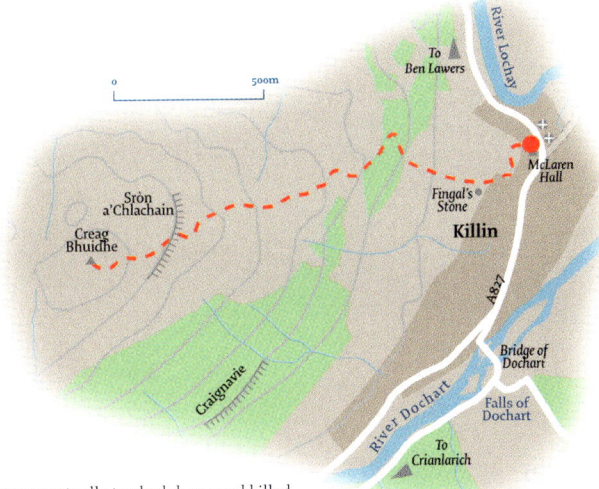

was eventually tracked down and killed. Some believe that Fingal gave his name to the town, 'Killin' being derived from the Gaelic *Chil-fhinn*, meaning 'Cell' or 'Church of Fingal'. However, it is also attributed to the more mundane *Cill fionn*, meaning 'White' or 'Fair Church'. After visiting the stone, return to the main path and go through a gate to head uphill towards the oakwoods and through a second gate.

Go over the stile and follow the path on its steep journey into the trees, before swinging back and emerging onto open moorland. This is a sheep-grazing area and dog owners should keep their dogs on a lead. The path continues to rise steeply, climbing up over a number of grassy knolls before reaching the first crag. From here, there are great views down over Killin and Loch Tay.

Another **two very steep** sections follow, where steps have been worn into the slope making the ascent easier. Finally, the top of Sron a'Chlachain, a crag with a small cairn, is gained. This is a fine viewpoint, and many people make this the end point of their walk. However, once you've got this far it is only a relatively short distance to the top of the higher summit of Creag Bhuidhe. The path dips slightly before making the steep, rocky climb, easing off before the broad summit. Here, you'll see three cairns, the largest on the far side of a stone wall marking the true summit at 510m. The views are superb in all directions, taking in many high mountains as well as the loch. The descent is by the same route with the toy town view of Killin getting larger with every step.

◂ Killin and Loch Tay from Creag Bhuidhe

Falls of Dochart to Acharn Woods

Distance 6km **Time** 2 hours
Terrain forestry tracks, gentle climb
Map OS Explorer OL48 **Access** buses to Killin from Crianlarich, Lochearnhead and Callander

This easy walk follows a section of the old Killin railway and part of the Rob Roy Way to explore Acharn Woods, a mix of native trees and commercial plantations. There is a gentle climb, with great views of the Tarmachan Ridge on the return.

Start from the southwest side of Killin, where the A827 squeezes the traffic over the tumbling rapids of the Falls of Dochart. On the far side is St Fillan's Mill, a reminder of times when Killin was an important centre for the linen trade. Flax was grown locally and spun in small mills like this before being woven into cloth by an army of home-based weavers.

From the Falls of Dochart Inn (strictly customer parking only; there is a public car park back in the centre of town) follow the main road past a long row of houses. Before you reach the war memorial, turn left across the road at the sign for Lochearnhead to pass between the end of the terraced bungalows and a more modern house on a track. Pass an information board and go through a gateway before turning right along the old railway line. This was an offshoot of the Callander to Oban line which arrived in Killin in 1886 and was responsible for the village moving away from the loch shore. The railway line actually went as far as the pier on Loch Tay, where a steamer made the onward journey to Kenmore. The railway closed in 1939 and much of the route is now part of a network of footpaths. Follow the old line as it plunges straight through woodland with open

◀ Falls of Dochart

fields on the right where deer can sometimes be seen grazing.

This section of the walk is part of the long-distance Rob Roy Way, which follows in the footsteps of the local hero and outlaw. It is also a haven for wildlife, particularly small birds, and flowers.

Continue on the railway line, passing the tennis court and buildings at Acharn on the right. The large pond in the next field is a good place to watch fish leaping at flies. Soon after this, go straight across a forestry track and carry on until another crossroads is reached. Turn left here and climb gently uphill following the sign for Lochearnhead.

As you gain height, there are views back across Glen Dochart to steep hillsides. Ignore a track off to the left and keep straight on at the next junction where the cycle route leaves to head right towards Lochearnhead. Turn at the next junction to join another forestry track. The route starts to descend with good views of the knobbly Tarmachan Ridge ahead. When you eventually meet a larger track and depot, bear left to follow this downhill to the start.

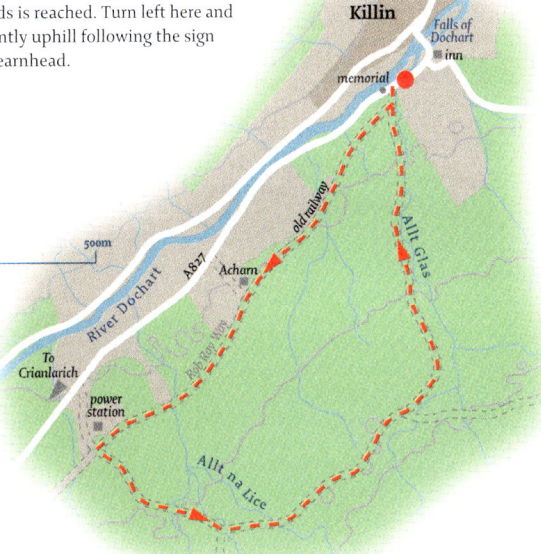

In the 1700s the position of Crieff on the boundary between the Highlands and the Lowlands made it a town of much importance. The famous Tryst, or annual fair, was held every October. At its heart was Scotland's most important cattle sale, to which Highland drovers brought around 30,000 beasts to market from all across the Highlands. The Tryst was eventually moved to Forfar, and by Victorian times Crieff had become a resort town and spa. The great size of the Crieff Hydro Hotel is a testament to its popularity. Built in 1868, it was originally operated on strict religious grounds with a fine of one penny imposed on anyone late for grace at mealtimes. The atmosphere is now more relaxed with many activities on offer. Crieff remains the second largest town in Perthshire.

Today, this area still enjoys a little of the advantages of both the Highlands and Lowlands, with the rich and fertile landscape of Strathearn – complete with the famous golf courses at Gleneagles – merging slowly into the wilder hills to the north and west. Strathearn is packed with small towns and villages, from the 'Lang Toun' of Auchterarder to attractive Comrie on the Highland Boundary Fault, then stretching west to lovely St Fillans on the shores of Loch Earn.

Crieff and Strathearn

1. **River Earn from Crieff to Muthill** 66
   Journey from market town to village along the peaceful banks of the Earn

2. **The Hosh and the Knock** 68
   Enjoy a sweeping perspective over Crieff, with the option to enjoy a dram or two along the way

3. **Comrie and the Deil's Cauldron** 70
   Visit the enchanting waterfalls on the Glen Lednock Circular with a detour to the monument above Comrie

4. **St Fillan's Hill** 72
   Climb this small rocky knoll to discover where the Celtic missionary set up shop in heathen Perthshire

5. **St Fillans view over Loch Earn** 74
   Climb above a lovely village and an underground powerhouse for spectacular views of Loch Earn

6. **Loop of Loch Freuchie** 76
   Set out from Amulree for a long but easygoing circuit up Glen Quaich

7. **Auchterarder Oak and Jubilee Walk** 78
   Explore the farmland around the Lang Toun with great Ochil views

8. **Around Ben Shee** 80
   Loop round Ben Shee on this waymarked circuit in beautiful Glen Devon

River Earn from Crieff to Muthill

Distance 10km **Time** 3 hours
Terrain good waymarked paths, muddy in places, minor roads **Map** OS Explorer OL47
Access Crieff is well served by buses; bus from Muthill to return

This lovely linear walk explores the resort town of Crieff before following the banks of the River Earn and a path through beautiful woodland to the conservation village of Muthill. There is a bus service back to Crieff.

Start from James Square in the centre of Crieff. The town has a colourful past, and you will be treading in the footsteps of Rob Roy MacGregor, Bonnie Prince Charlie and Robert Burns here. Perthshire's second largest settlement, Crieff grew as a droving town, with cattle driven from all over northern Scotland for sale to lowland buyers at its large trysts (markets). James Square was laid out in 1731 when the textile industry began to develop. After the arrival of the railway in the 1850s, Crieff became a fashionable spa and resort.

Follow the main street west towards Comrie, keeping straight ahead on Lodge Street (signposted for Stirling) when the Comrie road branches right. After passing the family of 'Leafy Coos' which represent the town's droving history, cross Burrell Street and continue downhill onto Drummawhandie Road. Carry on down a flight of steps to reach Sauchie Road and continue on the footpath (signposted for Muthill). Follow it through woodland, across a minor road and around the edge of the cemetery to reach a road. Turn right here onto Earnbank Road (River Earn Walk) and follow it to the busy road to Stirling, then turn right and cross the River Earn on the stone bridge.

Once across the river, take the second right onto Alichmore Lane. At a corner,

River Earn from Crieff to Muthill

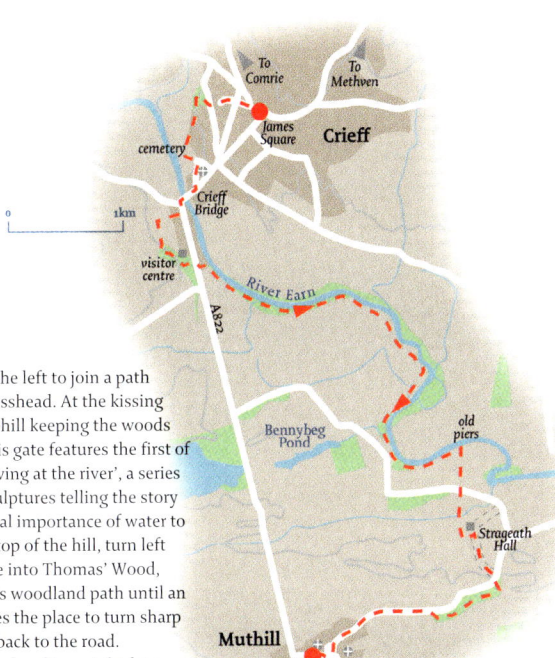

◂ The River Earn

leave this on the left to join a path signed for Crosshead. At the kissing gate, climb uphill keeping the woods to the left. This gate features the first of 'six hands waving at the river', a series of wooden sculptures telling the story of the historical importance of water to Crieff. At the top of the hill, turn left through a gate into Thomas' Wood, keeping to this woodland path until an arrow indicates the place to turn sharp left and drop back to the road.

Cross the road and turn right for a very short distance, then take the signed path to reach the riverside. Turn right along the riverbank before diverting onto an embankment. After returning to the riverside the path goes through a number of gates before passing the buildings at Templemill. Continue meandering along to reach the rusting piers of the former viaduct over the river and turn right to follow the old railway line (which can get overgrown at times).

Carry on through two gates and under a bridge, then go through a gate and turn left towards Strageath Hall where the driveway steers you right to meet a minor road. Join this to the right before soon turning left into Sallyardoch Wood and picking up the yellow waymarked path through the trees.

When the path meets a minor road turn left for Muthill. The pretty village centre of Muthill is well worth exploring before you catch the return bus, especially the ancient kirkyard with the ruin of a 15th-century church and a 12th-century belltower.

The Hosh and the Knock

Distance 10km **Time** 3 hours
Terrain paths, tracks and minor roads, can be muddy in places; one steep section
Map OS Explorer OL47 **Access** Crieff is well served by buses

This figure-of-eight walk climbs the Knock for a sweeping view of mountain, moor and strath, as well as exploring the woods and riverside of the Hosh.

Start from the Knock car park, which sits high above Crieff off Ferntower Road. (Head for Crieff Hydro, then follow signs for Action Glen.) To take in the Hosh loop first, continue along the road, keeping left at a fork to stay on the tarmac road for the outdoor activity centre. Ignore a track off left and pass the reception area, then go straight ahead through a parking area. Continue on a rougher track (signposted for The Hosh) which soon gives views across lower Glen Turret as it descends with a hedge on your left and trees on the right. Ignore a path off left and follow the track as it swings left.

At a signposted junction, go right to cross a wooden bridge, bearing left on the far side and left again at the road. Soon after Turret Bridge is Glenturret Distillery. Turn left into the distillery car park and go behind the buildings to reach a wooden footbridge over the Turret.

On the other side, a path goes left and then swings right to climb to a junction. Turn sharp right here (signposted for Comrie Road) and then left (signposted for Culcrieff) at the next junction to zigzag steeply through the trees. When you meet a lane, turn left again and, just before the self-catering lodges, take a path on the right. Go straight across one lane onto the track opposite. Now signed as the cinder path for Crieff Hydro Hotel, the route runs along a natural balcony, passing a stone-built well, dated 1874. The water here was said to have healing properties and it is what made Crieff

THE HOSH AND THE KNOCK

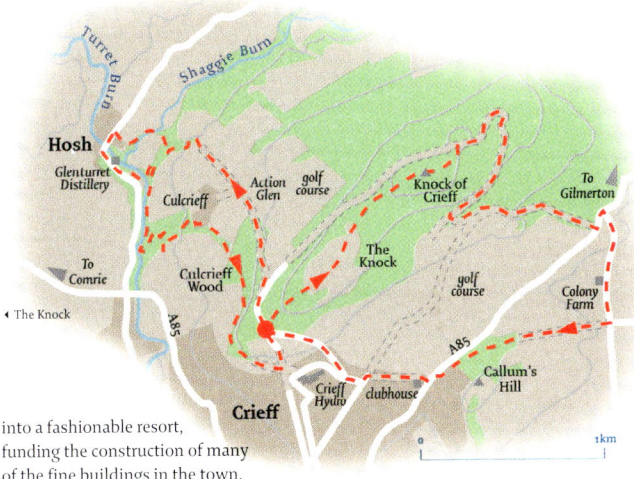

◀ The Knock

into a fashionable resort, funding the construction of many of the fine buildings in the town.

As you follow the terrace, you can enjoy sweeping views along Strathearn and over Crieff itself. Join a tarmac lane and, just before a gap in a high wall, with the Hydro ahead, turn left up a steep path. This accompanies a wall as it climbs the field to reach another set of self-catering houses and the Knock car park just beyond.

To complete the second loop of this route, cross the road and tackle the Knock by starting up the wide path beside the information board. The route climbs steeply to emerge from the trees at a viewpoint indicator. Follow the constructed path from here along the spine of the hill and then keep ahead at a crosspaths. The path then bears left at a fence; go through the gate here and on through trees to reach the true summit of the Knock. Continue ahead, now downhill, ignoring a mountain bike track off right.

Eventually a track is reached where you turn right to pass the millennium cairn. Just beyond this, turn left onto a track and then left again onto a path to almost double back. The path runs alongside the golf course to a gate and track, part of a road built by General Wade. Go straight over this onto the track to the A85. Cross the road with care, following it to the left briefly before turning right onto a minor road signed for Highlandman Loan.

At the junction after Colony Farm, turn right onto a grassy track, crossing farmland to reach a wood of beech, oak and birch. Cross the A85 again, where the path skirts just left of the golf course and right of the clubhouse. Where it meets a track, turn left to reach the end of Ferntower Road, then turn right for the climb towards the Hydro, taking the road on the right before you reach the hotel.

Comrie and the Deil's Cauldron

Distance 7.5km **Time** 3 hours
Terrain path, minor road, avoidable steep section **Map** OS Explorer OL47
Access buses to Comrie from Crieff

This excellent circular walk visits the Deil's Cauldron, a tree-clad amphitheatre where the River Lednock cascades down a rocky gorge – with an optional climb to the Melville Monument above Comrie.

Start from School Road car park between the two right-angled bends on the main road in Comrie. Most of the route is signposted as the Glen Lednock Circular Walk. Turn right along the main road, walking straight on at the sharp bend to follow the road towards Glen Lednock. Where the road bends left, go through an old stone gateway onto a signed path; this meanders through beech woodland, close to the River Lednock.

To view the first feature on this walk, the Little Cauldron, a smaller path takes you down some steps on the right where you can see the river cascade down a low rocky gully into a deep pool, before looping back to the main route. This now climbs high above the water as it draws near to the road; stay on the path.

As the sides of the glen steepen, the trail soon crosses a wooden walkway with the drops fenced off. At the far end, a flight of steps leads you down to the viewpoint for the Deil's Cauldron itself, where the river emerges from a rock-walled gorge with a double cascade into a wide pool. The verdant foliage, deep ravine and crashing water give this spot a powerful atmosphere. From the Cauldron, climb the wooden staircase on the right to the road. As before, bear right to stay on the path alongside rather than on the road itself.

The visit to Dun More and the Melville Monument involves a very steep ascent, and can be bypassed by simply continuing along the road, rejoining the route further on. However, the effort is rewarded with splendid views. A signed path directs you to the left after a short distance. This climbs unrelentingly uphill at first, easing off for a

◀ The Maam Road

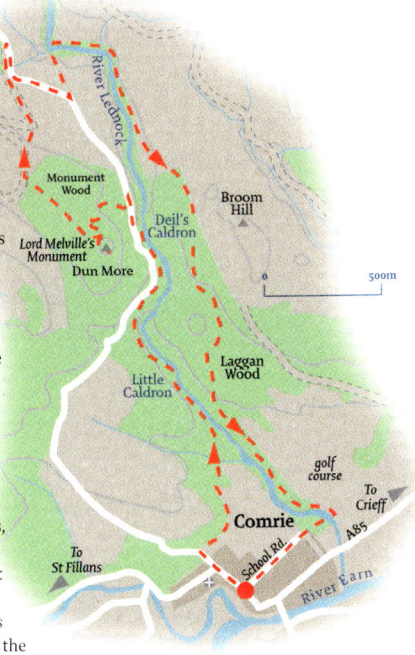

section before swinging left across rough ground for the final push to the top, joining a path coming in from the right. The tall obelisk was erected to celebrate the achievements of Henry Dundas, First Viscount Melville who rose through the ranks of the Scottish legal establishment to become Solicitor General in 1766 before turning to politics. He was the last person to be impeached by the House of Lords in 1806 after being accused of improper use of funds during his time in charge of the Admiralty – though he was later acquitted. From the monument are great views southwards to the Ochils, while further right is a glimpse of Loch Earn, with Ben Vorlich and Stuc a'Chroin high above.

From Dun More, retrace your steps briefly but keep on the main path to the left. This eventually reaches a large gate where it joins an old hill track known as the Maam Road. Turn right to pass a wooden seat with an outlook up Glen Lednock. The descent is made via a looping zigzag track with options for shortcuts down to Monument Road. When you reach the tarmac road, turn right to find a grassy track (signposted for Laggan Wood) to the left. This is where you rejoin the main route if the ascent of Dun More has been omitted. Keep right to cross a wooden footbridge and take the path downstream to the right.

After a stile, climb a small flight of steps and turn right at a wider path with views towards the Melville Monument. Climb to a bench and go through a wooden gate into an area of woodland. Continue to a waymarked junction and turn right down through mature woods. Keep right at a fork to head more steeply towards the water, eventually joining an all-abilities path. Keep straight ahead here to reach the river at a bench and weir. Follow the path downstream to cross over a footbridge and join the route of the old railway straight ahead behind the main street to the start.

St Fillan's Hill

Distance 6.25km **Time** 2 hours 30
Terrain easy tracks, boggy path, steep and rocky final ascent **Map** OS Explorer OL47
Access bus to St Fillans from Crieff

Starting from the delightful village of St Fillans, this walk crosses flat ground and a golf course to reach the ruin of a pre-Reformation chapel before climbing a craggy hill named after the venerated Irish missionary. The summit was also the site of the ancient Pictish stronghold of Dundurn, a strategically important fort which guarded Strathearn from the marauding Scots of Dalriada.

There is parking off the A85 in the middle of St Fillans, on the left soon after the shop if approaching from Comrie.

Start the walk by facing Loch Earn and turning left to cross an arched footbridge over the River Earn. Turn left on the far side to follow a path downstream. When it reaches a minor road turn left, soon passing a weir which is part of the St Fillans hydro-power scheme.

At a bend in the road just before a stone bridge, turn sharp right onto a track leading across the golf course. Take care and give way to any golfers hitting their drives across the track. The rocky knoll of Dundurn can be seen clearly ahead across the fairways. Follow the track around a sharp bend and at the next bend, with a house visible ahead, turn left through a gate onto another track to aim directly towards Dundurn.

St Fillan's Hill

◀ View from Dundurn Hill

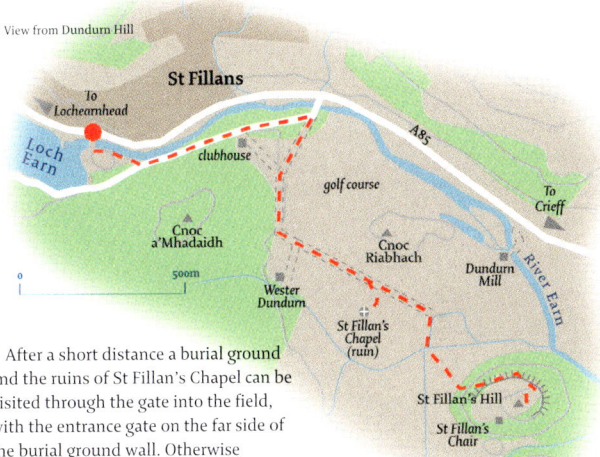

After a short distance a burial ground and the ruins of St Fillan's Chapel can be visited through the gate into the field, with the entrance gate on the far side of the burial ground wall. Otherwise continue on the track, heading towards the conifers. Pass the gates to the waterworks and go through the gate ahead to enter the field in front of Dundurn.

This field can be very boggy; keep your feet dry by following the top of a grassy bank just to the right and then cross a burn either on stepping stones or a makeshift bridge just to the left. Aim diagonally left to reach a stile at the foot of Dundurn. Climb this and follow an indistinct path which starts to climb round the slopes to the left. The path, which can be overgrown with bracken in high summer, climbs steeply, following grass to the left side of a scree slope for one section. As the path reaches the far side of the hill there are good views down Strathearn. The path peters out but keep heading steeply up and around the hill to reach the flat summit.

The prominent rock outcrop is known as St Fillan's Chair and it is thought the monk from Munster based himself here in a hermit's cell while he went about converting the local Picts to Christianity. No remains of this cell have been found, however, and there is very little visible evidence of the Pictish fort which once stood here guarding the borderland between Scots and Picts. Nevertheless the site is a protected Scheduled Ancient Monument in recognition of its national importance to Picts and Christians.

Dundurn has sheer rocks on most sides so the best way down is to return the same way and then go back across the muddy field. Follow the track towards St Fillans. Once at the minor road, retrace the outward route to the footbridge, or instead cross the roadbridge and follow the pavement of the A85, passing some attractive cottages on the way.

St Fillans view over Loch Earn

Distance 6km **Time** 2 hours
Terrain track, road with pavement
Map OS Explorer OL47 **Access** bus to
St Fillans from Crieff

A steep climb through the woods above St Fillans is rewarded with fine views over Loch Earn to Ben Vorlich, returning through oakwoods and past the pretty cottages of St Fillans, beautifully situated on the shores of the loch.

This route begins from a lochside lay-by at the west end of St Fillans, opposite the bus shelter. Take the lane that climbs west from behind the shelter and pass the entrance to the hydro-electric power station. This walk's objective – the viewpoint – is the site of the surge shaft where water tumbles into the ground to drive the turbines in an underground cavern far below. The lane passes a couple of houses as it continues to rise and then doubles back at a sharp right-hand bend.

Ignore the path left down onto the disused railway line, instead crossing the bridge over it. Pass through an iron gate to head through birch and conifer woods, ignoring the gate into the woods at the next bend. Swing left on the rising track, avoiding another gated track on the right (this is used on the return). Further on, where the track forks, bear right. Leave the forest at a gate and head for the flat area ahead. Take the left-hand fork here for a final steep ascent to the fenced-off surge shaft. There are lovely views along the whole length of Loch Earn and over to Ben Vorlich, one of the most popular Munros.

Retrace the outward route as far as the third gate and turn left through it to follow the track to a seat with a view over Loch Earn. Descend a series of zigzags on

St Fillans view over Loch Earn

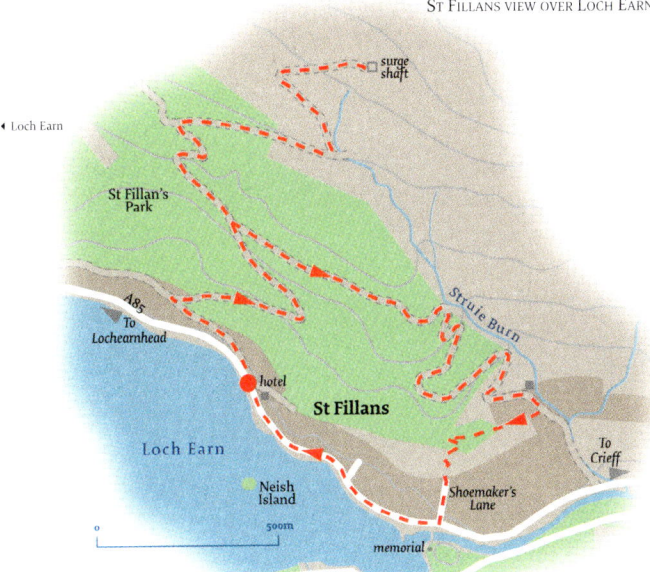

the track and pass a pair of cottages to go through a gap in the old railway line. Turn right on the multi-use surfaced path and follow it above the village until you reach a signed surfaced path leading off on the left. This goes past a playpark to reach Shoemaker's Lane, which is followed down to the main road.

It is worth making a short detour across the road and pedestrian bridge opposite, bearing right to the village war memorial for the superb views up the loch. Otherwise, continue along the pavement to eventually return to the start of the walk.

Just offshore is Neish Island, once the site of Loch Earn Castle and a bloody episode in the area's history. In the 15th and 16th centuries, the MacNeishes were a clan notorious for cattle and property raiding. At the Battle of Glen Boultachan in 1522, they were routed by the MacNabs and the few survivors retreated to Loch Earn Castle. The clan regrouped and by 1612 had staged an audacious attack on the MacNabs as they returned with supplies from Crieff. The vengeful MacNabs hauled a boat over the mountains from Loch Tay, rowed to the castle and attacked, returning triumphant to Loch Tay with their bounty – including a number of severed heads. Today, the island is a peaceful wildlife haven and nothing remains of the castle.

Loop of Loch Freuchie

Distance 12.5km **Time** 3 hours
Terrain track, quiet minor road
Map OS Explorer 379 **Access** no public transport to the start

Loch Freuchie lies in remote Glen Quaich, with good opportunities to watch birds and enjoy the peace on a longer but straightforward circular hike.

The walk starts from the scattered hamlet of Amulree, known for its striking white church. From the north end of Amulree, where the A822 crosses the River Braan, take the private road signed as a footpath to Kenmore. This soon passes Lochan Cottages and bears left to pass Lochan Lodge, becoming a rougher track as it crosses a cattle grid and heads around the north side of Glen Quaich.

This route is part of the long-distance Rob Roy Way, which runs for 148km from Drymen to Pitlochry on paths and tracks used by the outlaw Rob Roy Macgregor in the 17th and 18th centuries. Beyond the farm, the track skirts the north side of Loch Freuchie. Across the water, the Rob Roy Way can be made out coming down the steep-sided cleft of Glen Lochan.

Pass a cottage, a lone Scots pine and another cattle grid to cross open farmland. When the track forks, keep on the lower branch and climb gently between some drystane dykes. As Loch Freuchie comes into view, the remains of a crannog, an artificial island which would have provided a safe house during the Iron Age, can be seen. According to legend, the island was originally inhabited by a fearsome dragon. As is usual with these stories, a foolish young man named Fraoch followed the request of a lady to gather rowan berries from the island. He managed to complete the task and evaded the dragon, but the lady then insisted that

◂ Loch Freuchie

nothing would please her except to be presented with the rowan tree itself. Alas, on his return visit, the young lad uprooted his prize only to be ripped limb from limb by the awakened dragon. Needless to say, there is no archaeological or historical evidence to support the story. Although they didn't help Fraoch, rowan trees are still regarded as symbols of good luck.

Continuing on the track and passing through the gates, scattered woodland replaces grazing land. You'll soon see the head of the loch, with good views up Glen Quaich. The farm here has worked to increase the biodiversity of the habitat, making this a good spot for birdwatching.

The track now passes the ruins of an old settlement, a spot which can be muddy underfoot, and curves down towards Turrerich Farm. Pass to the left of the farmyard and follow the track round the head of the loch. There is a lovely old stone bridge over the River Quaich before the track reaches the road.

Turn left and follow this minor road all the way back to Amulree, with good views over the water for much of the journey. Although a tiny village today, this was a thriving community prior to the 1800s when land was cleared to make way for sheep. On one single day, 300 crofters left on the same ship bound for Canada. After a three-month voyage they settled in part of Ontario, naming their new townships Amulree and Glenquaich.

Auchterarder Oak and Jubilee Walk

Distance 7km **Time** 2 hours 30
Terrain paths, tracks, minor roads
Map OS Explorer OL47 **Access** buses to Auchterarder from Perth and Crieff; train station at nearby Gleneagles

Explore Auchterarder on this easy route through the centre of town and on the Provost's Walk, a footpath near the Lochy Burn and Ruthven Water, with good views of the Ochils and surrounding farmland.

Auchterarder is strung out along its long main street, giving it the nickname of the *Lang Toun*. The town was originally an important centre for the weaving, distilling and malting industries, before being sidelined by the growth of Crieff in the 1700s. It became a Royal Burgh in 1200 and was often host to royalty, generals and nobility. With the arrival of the railway in 1848 and the development of the first golf course soon after, Auchterarder began to shape itself into the present-day centre for golfing holidays. Nearby Gleneagles was built as a resort by the Caledonian Railway Company, boasting two 18-hole courses. The resort now has three championship-standard courses as well as another of nine holes.

Start the walk from the Crown Wynd car park off the High Street, just west of the Aytoun Hall and clocktower. From here, head left along the main street, passing several independent shops and cafés. After a short distance, turn right along Castleton Road to follow this as it leads out into farmland. When you reach the small settlement of Castleton, turn left along a lane (signposted Footpath to Oak Walk) to pass Lower Borland Park Farm.

At the end of the track, take the footpath to the left of the house and cross a small bridge and a stile to enter the oakwood. Head left and follow the winding path up

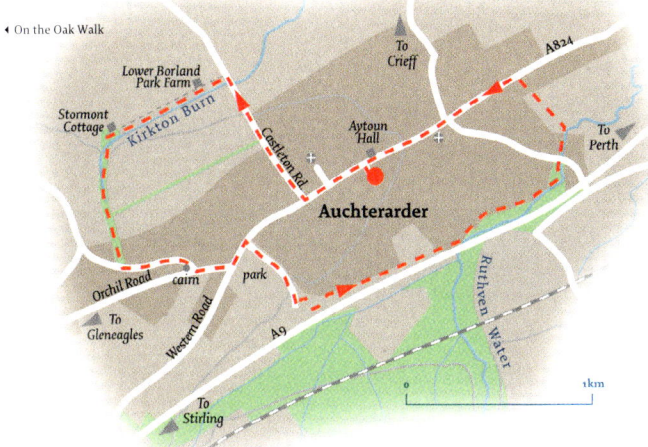

On the Oak Walk

through the belt of mixed woodland, going over a couple of small bridges along the way. When the path emerges onto Tullibardine Road, turn left to join Orchil Road. A stone cairn sits at the entrance to the Cairn Lodge Hotel here, built to commemorate Queen Victoria's jubilee.

Turn left along Orchil Road, crossing Western Road when you reach it and heading left by the park for a short distance. At the corner of the park, turn right towards the recycling centre. When the road bends right take a path on the left to continue ahead. This path winds down through mature trees before reaching a junction with another tarmac path.

Turn left here and continue between Auchterarder and the A9 road for 1.5km. Ignore the houses on the left initially, and later a turning on the left (signed Rossie Place), always continuing ahead.

Eventually the path emerges at the end of a minor road. Go straight across, taking the narrow path to the left side of the Ruthven Water. Note the fish ladder in the weir on your right. Keep the water on your right as you follow the clear path (ignore a left turn for the High Street), eventually reaching a minor road. Continue straight ahead, passing some attractive cottages.

Ignore another turning on the left ('Black Road'), keeping ahead until a road is reached. Go straight across to follow the lane towards Glenruthven Mill. Continue along the path past the mill and go up a flight of steps to farmland with open views back to the Ochils. The path continues between fields to meet the main road into Auchterarder. Turn left here and follow the road all the way back to the middle of the High Street.

Around Ben Shee

Distance 9.75km **Time** 3 hours 30
Terrain waymarked track and moorland paths, faint and boggy in places
Map OS Explorer 366 **Access** no public transport to the start

This popular moorland route in rural Glen Devon has a proper 'get away from it all' feel with wide open views and expansive skies as well as reservoirs, woodland and plenty of chances to spot wildlife, especially birds of prey.

Start from the Woodland Trust car park at the foot of Glensherup in Glen Devon and follow the waymarked path (Ben Shee Loop) which gently climbs up beside the burn. At the forestry track turn right. After 1km turn right onto a path to head towards the Lower Glendevon Reservoir.

The path descends to a fork: keep left at first to avoid an eroded path straight to the dam; instead take the next right branch to zigzag back to the dam and cross its grassy top.

At the far side the path bends left and then up to a gate and track. Turn left and keep right on a path to skirt a cabin, rejoining the grassy track afterwards. This heads through a gate and up the glen through large patches of regenerating woodland. Some 1.5 million native trees have been planted in this area as part of a scheme to encourage native birch woodland, with the eventual aim of re-wilding the glen. After another 1km the path starts climbing and becomes rougher underfoot, eventually reaching the bealach between Ben Shee to the right and the rest

Around Ben Shee

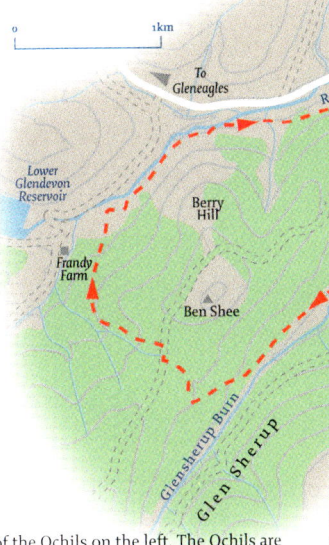

of the Ochils on the left. The Ochils are bald, steep and rolling hills with slopes of grass and bracken and, as height is gained, the feeling of remoteness increases. This is an excellent area to look out for osprey, buzzards, hen harrier, peregrine falcon, merlin and red kites.

The rough path meets a grassier one; turn right along it for 100m until a signpost indicates a left turn. You can detour straight ahead to reach the 516m summit of Ben Shee, a lovely viewpoint. Otherwise take the left path which descends with views to the Upper Glendevon Reservoirs. The Glendevon Reservoirs were constructed by German prisoners of war during the First World War to supply water to Dunfermline and Rosyth in Fife. Although the path can be squelchy underfoot in places it passes through a good mix of woodlands with views to the reservoirs in between.

Eventually you reach a signed junction; turn right here (signposted Glendevon Reservoirs Trail & Loop Paths) to head gradually downhill, crossing some small burns. Near the bottom of the glen the path keeps to the south side of the main burn, with the road and fish hatchery in view on the far side. Although often wet, the path is easy to make out and there are occasional waymarkers as it meanders down Glen Devon.

After a metal gate keep just to the right of a forestry plantation as the path becomes much fainter. Keep straight on across open grazing land, climbing very slightly before descending, aiming towards the two houses at Wester Glensherup. Reach the road just to the right of these houses and turn right to follow the surfaced road back up towards the reservoir and rejoin the outward route, turning left to cross the dam. On the far side climb up the zigzag path and turn left along the forestry track to return to the car park.

◀ Looking towards Lower Glendevon Reservoir

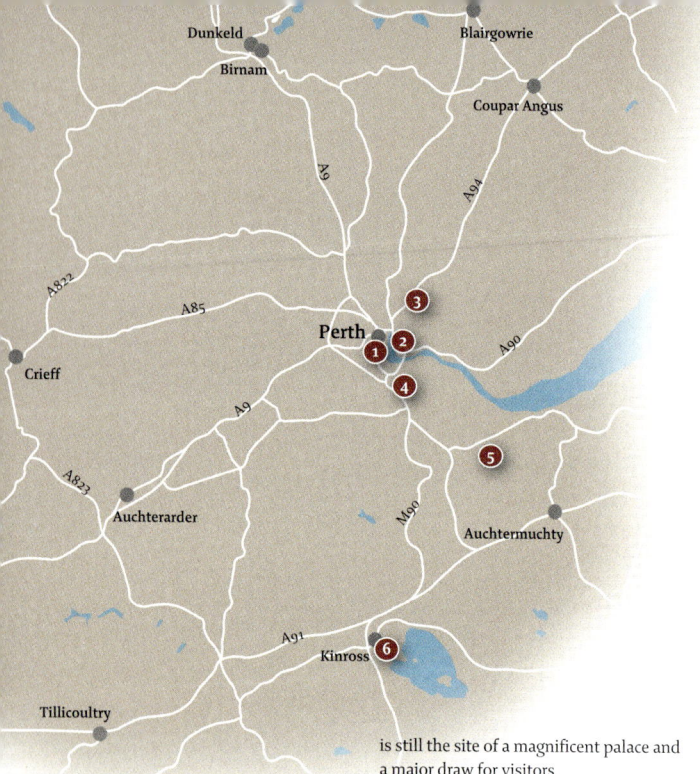

Perth well deserves its title as the Fair City. The capital of Perthshire enjoys a splendid location astride the mighty Tay, the country's grandest river. It has scores of fine Georgian buildings, a vibrant range of shops and an array of parks and gardens, including the large grassy Inches alongside the river. The kings of Scotland were crowned for centuries at nearby Scone on the famous Stone of Destiny. Today, the stone itself is on display in Perth but Scone is still the site of a magnificent palace and a major draw for visitors.

The area has many gentle hills crowned with monuments and historical remains. These offer excellent objectives for walks, where fascinating local history is matched by extensive views over town and country.

To the south is the town of Kinross, once the seat of a separate county, close to the shores of Loch Leven, the largest loch in the Lowlands. This is an important nature reserve and a fantastic place to visit for birdwatching.

St Matthew's Church and the River Tay ▶

Perth and Kinross

1 **A tour of the Fair City** 84
Explore the art and history at the heart of Perth on this short city walk packed full of interest

2 **Kinnoull Tower from Perth** 86
Climb to the spectacular site of a folly inspired by the castles of the Rhine, and detour to Branklyn Garden

3 **The Scone circular** 88
Pay a visit to the hilltop monuments over this historic planned village with fine views to Perth

4 **Moncreiffe Hill and the old fort** 90
Weave through a beautiful woodland reserve to the site of an Iron Age fort

5 **The Round Tower and Abernethy Glen** 92
Enjoy a short circular from an ancient village that was once home to Pictish kings, nestling in the Ochils

6 **Loch Leven and Kinross House** 94
Don't forget your binoculars on this visit to one of the most important wildfowl sites in Britain

PERTH AND KINROSS

A tour of the Fair City

Distance 7km **Time** 2 hours
Terrain parkland, city streets
Map OS Explorer 369 **Access** Perth is well served by buses, coaches and trains

Explore the historic Fair City and the beautiful North Inch parkland beside the Tay, with opportunities to extend the walk time by calling in at galleries, shops and museums along the way.

Begin from the car park on Shore Road at the north corner of South Inch, part of the Inches which were traditionally used for cattle grazing, linen drying and horse racing. From the entrance, cross Marshall Place and go past the historic domed waterworks building, then take the steps up to the railway and footbridge over the Tay, high above Moncreiffe Island with its golf course and allotments.

On the far side, turn left to enjoy the riverside public art trail as you shadow the Tay through Bellwood Park to reach Millais' Viewpoint, a carved stone frame with a view of the Sheriff Court across the water. Continue through Rodney Gardens to pass under Queen's Bridge before eventually emerging on Commercial Street, where you bear left. Cross West Bridge Street and head across Perth Bridge.

Continue along the pavement on the far side to the statue of Prince Albert in the robes of a Knight of the Thistle. Turn right towards the river, passing a statue of a soldier and a girl and the regimental obelisk of the Perthshire Volunteers, then go left along the riverside with great views across the Tay. The path finally arcs left to return on the far side of the Inches, passing Bell's Sports Centre and the Black Watch Museum, housed in Balhousie Castle.

Soon leave the park and go left along

A tour of the Fair City

◀ An illuminated St John's Kirk

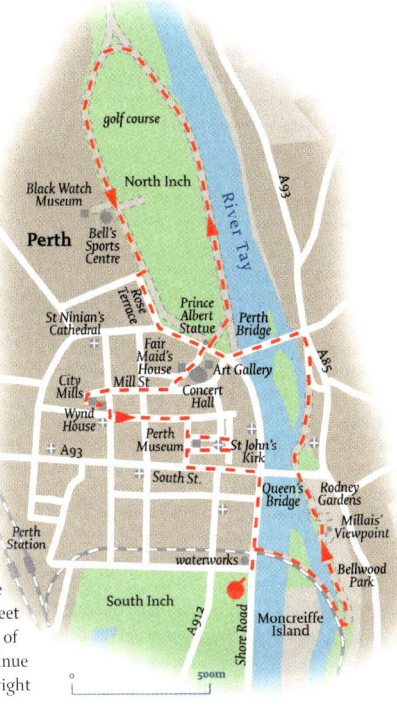

Georgian Rose Terrace with a rooftop statue of Britannia. Cross Atholl Street and go left past Atholl Crescent, then right into North Port. On the left is the concert hall with Perth Art Gallery next to it. On the right is the Fair Maid's House, the oldest secular building in Perth, which was renamed after Walter Scott's popular novel of 1828. Beyond, Curfew Row, once a medieval street of tanners and malters, leads through to Mill Street, where you turn right.

Cross Kinnoull and South Methven Streets to follow the mill lade past the old city mill. Head around the far side, noting the stone tower in the façade of Wynd House ahead; go through the narrow passage here to emerge on South Methven Street and turn right for the remaining walls of St Paul's Church. Cross over and continue down the High Street before turning right into King Edward Street.

Perth Museum, home of the Stone of Destiny, used in the coronation of British kings and queens for centuries, is up ahead. Beyond is St John's Kirk, Perth's oldest building, which dates in part from 1100. Follow St John's Place back up the other side of the church, where you'll see a sign for Fleshers Vennel, named after the butchers that once traded in this area.

Back on King Edward Street, head left and turn left again on South Street.

Continue back towards the Tay, passing Perth's oldest hotel, The Salutation, with its painted Black Watch figures. Eventually the Tay is reached once more. There was a harbour on the river here when Perth was an important trading port from the 12th century. Don't cross Queen's Bridge; instead turn right along the riverside, with views across the Tay to the wooded slopes of Kinnoull Hill, and pass under the railway line to return to the car park.

Kinnoull Tower from Perth

Distance 6.5km **Time** 2 hours 30
Terrain roads and paths, steep sections
Map OS Explorer 369 **Access** Perth is well served by buses, coaches and trains

From the centre of Perth, Kinnoull Hill gives no hint of the drama of its clifftop escarpment high above the Tay. The walk time can be shortened by starting from the Quarry car park off Corsiehill Road, or can be combined in spring and summer with a visit to Branklyn Garden.

Begin the walk from South Inch car park, just south of the city centre, or simply turn right from the bottom of the High Street where it reaches the Tay. Climb the steps to cross the viaduct/footbridge opposite for good views of Perth along the river.

On the opposite side, go straight ahead to ascend a flight of steps to the main Dundee Road. Carefully cross this busy road, and head right for a short distance before branching left by the sign for the National Trust for Scotland's Branklyn Garden. Originally this, the Barnhill area of Perth, was dedicated to nurseries growing soft fruit. Dorothy and John Renton purchased one orchard here in 1922 and filled it with plants grown from seed gathered during early plant-hunting expeditions to China and the Himalayas. This small 'haven' is open in summer, but if you're not visiting then turn left again by the sign for Kinnoull Hill to climb a steep lane, straight over a crossroads and past fine buildings. Where the main lane turns left, head right onto a track. Take the next left turn at the corner of the Kinnoull Hill Woodland Park. The track climbs past

Kinnoull Tower from Perth

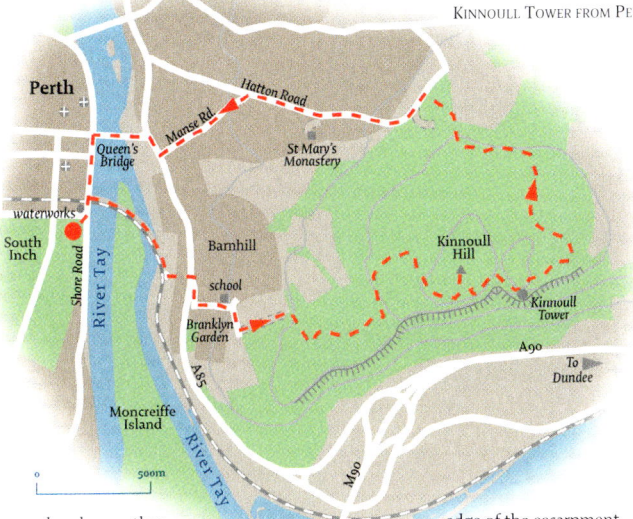

a modern house, then continues as a footpath. Keep on the main path when it curves right into the woods. There are many junctions; just stay on the main route which is marked in orange. Eventually it curves left below a steeper slope, and a fork is reached opposite a picnic bench. Bear right here, climbing through the trees to eventually reach a stone table on the escarpment with views over the Tay. The summit trig point can be reached by a short detour left from here, but the walk continues on the orange path, soon turning right then left to keep by the escarpment.

The high and dangerous cliffs on the right are partly obscured by the trees. Occasional gaps permit dizzying views down to the A90 far below, with the Lomond Hills and Fife beyond. Kinnoull Tower appears, dramatically, on the very edge of the escarpment.

Built as a folly in the 18th century, the tower was inspired by the castles along the Rhine in Germany. From here, the escarpment path continues to give expansive views, then swings left and soon reaches a junction. Keep left here, leaving the orange waymarked route temporarily. The marked trail soon rejoins from the left. Continue to another junction and turn right. Ignore the path left for the car park and continue to a picnic area.

Fork left here on a grassy path before reaching a tarmac road with a parking lay-by. Turn left to pass the neo-Gothic building of St Mary's Monastery and at the next crossroads go left down the narrow road which emerges on Dundee Road. Turn right, then left for Queen's Bridge, which you cross back to the city centre.

◀ Kinnoull Tower and the Tay

The Scone circular

Distance 9km **Time** 3 hours **Terrain** paths with one steep moorland section, minor roads **Map** OS Explorer 369
Access bus to Scone from Perth

This circular walk, created to celebrate the bicentenary of Scone being moved from its original position near Scone Palace, climbs to a folly and the Lynedoch Obelisk with extensive views, completing the loop by a wander through woodland, a golf course and the village itself.

The village of Scone (pronounced 'skoon') once stood close to the present position of Scone Palace. In 1805 the village was relocated, the Old Church being moved stone by stone to its new home at the southern end of the village. The walk begins from the car park near this church, signposted for the David Douglas Memorial from the main road.

Douglas was responsible for bringing many plants to Europe from the Americas, including the Sitka Spruce and the Douglas Fir – which was named in his honour. He was born in Scone and started his career as an apprentice gardener at the palace, but died in Hawaii, aged 35, after falling into a trap and being fatally gored by a wild bull.

Passing the church, head along Burnside to the Scone Arms. Use the crossing to go over the main Perth Road, and turn left. After a short distance, turn right onto Den Road and keep ahead, ignoring the footbridge to the children's play area. When the route ahead leads into a private driveway, turn right over a footbridge and follow the path into the wooded Den of Scone. The main path leads through a lovely area of mature trees and over a smaller bridge. Keep right as the pathway rises, turning left onto a minor road to continue the climb.

Just before the grand gateway to Bonhard House, turn right along a path (signposted for MacDuff's Monument). Go through another gate and woodland before turning left onto a road. Pass the

THE SCONE CIRCULAR

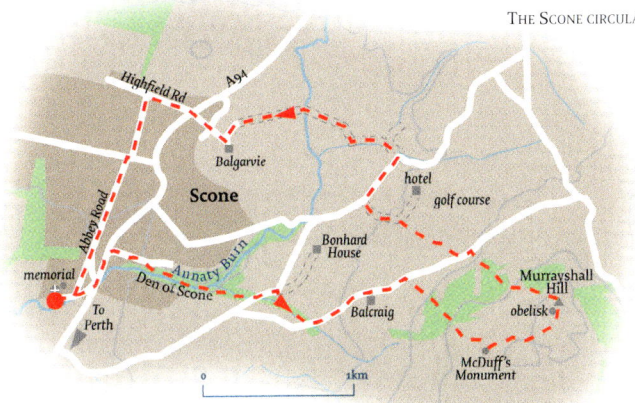

impressive eagle gateposts at Balcraig, continue for another 300m, then turn right up a waterworks track. After a gate the track swings right; keep ahead on a path that climbs steeply through trees. There is a boggy section through gorse before the path emerges at McDuff's Monument, built as a folly in the 1780s.

Continue along the path that swings left, soon coming alongside a fence. Follow this to the right to a gate and then pass through, continuing to reach the Lynedoch Obelisk, visible on the next hill to the left. Keep an eye out for deer and birds of prey on this stretch. The obelisk was erected in 1853 in memory of Lord Lynedoch who fought with Wellington to break the siege of Càdiz in the 1811 Battle of Barossa.

Follow a narrow path to the left; it forks but both branches rejoin. When it meets a grass track go straight across; there are red waymarkers. When the path meets a golf course track, turn left along it and soon bear right (red waymarker) to pass to the right of the 8th/16th tee. Continue down until you reach a road, then turn left along it briefly. Take the next path off right and ignore a footbridge to keep ahead, then turn left at the main golf course track, continuing down the side of the fairway. When you reach the tarmac driveway to Murrayshall continue to the road and turn right to a bend, where you follow a track left through farmland and past the ruins of the Mill of Bonhard. Once on the road near Balgarvie, turn left, then right towards Scone. Cross the first road and then the main A94 into Highfield Road.

This leads to Lynedoch Road, where you go left and, at the bottom, right and then left into Abbey Road, beside the Robert Douglas Park. Douglas, another Scone man, discovered pectin, the substance that makes jam set, and left much of his fortune to benefit the community when he died. Abbey Road takes you all the way through New Scone, past the Robert Douglas Memorial Institute: a right turn at the bottom leads to the car park at the start.

◂ McDuff's Monument

Moncreiffe Hill and the old fort

Distance 8km **Time** 2 hours 30
Terrain waymarked forestry tracks, path to summit **Map** OS Explorer 369
Access no public transport to the start

An excellent circular walk explores this beautiful Woodland Trust site in the countryside between Perth and Bridge of Earn. There are grand views over Perth, the Ochils and Fife from the summit.

There is limited parking at the start of this walk. To reach it, take the minor road heading east from just north of Bridge of Earn, passing under the M90. After just over 1.5km, a sign for Moncreiffe Hill indicates a bumpy track on the left, which leads to a small parking area just before a gate. You'll find a map of the walks here. This route follows a mix of the longer yellow route but also uses part of the blue sculpture trail and detours to reach the largest hillfort, Moredun.

Go through the gate and follow the main track, which rises slightly through attractive mixed woodland, home to deer and many species of birds. Ignore the waymarked route off to the right and carry on to eventually come close to the noisy M90. Just when it seems the track might be bound for the motorway itself, it ends and the walk bears right on a path climbing deeper into the woods. After looping round to the right in a clearer area and going uphill past a small pond, you come to a junction. Bear left, following the yellow marker posts to find a bench on the left at the very edge of the woods with a good view towards Perth.

Keep right at the next junction, leaving the yellow route again, to continue the ascent through the woods to another viewpoint bench. Keep right at the next junction and follow the path to eventually reach the foot of a steep grassy dome. This

◀ Perth from Moncreiffe Hill

is Moredun Top, the true summit of Moncreiffe Hill and the site of an ancient fort. To detour to the top, avoid the steep eroded path opposite and instead take the path to the left of the hill for a more gradual ascent as it spirals round to eventually reach the summit.

The top is encircled by a grassy bank, which is all that remains of an Iron Age fort. The walls of the fort were made of vitrified stone, rocks heated to such a high temperature that they melted and fused together. How such a high temperature was reached and why it was done are still a mystery to archaeologists. The summit is marked by a small cairn and has terrific views, especially over Perth and the Tay to the north, backed by the first hills of the Highlands. Slightly further round the summit edge is a stone rainwater basin thought to be associated with the fort. From here, the M90 can be seen snaking away south towards the central belt.

Return to the main path and bear left to follow yellow and red waymarkers through the forest, which for this section mainly consists of conifers. Ignore the path (also waymarked in yellow) off to the right and keep to the longer path as it runs along the top of a wooded escarpment for one section, giving great views of the Ochils. Finally, the path curves to the right and drops back to the outward route. Turn left here to return to the gate and the start.

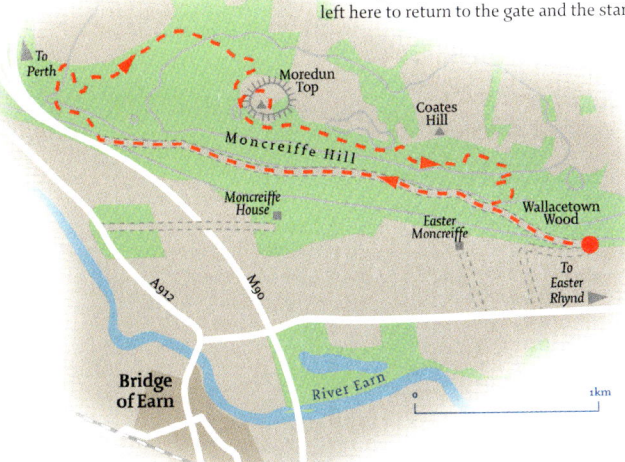

The Round Tower and Abernethy Glen

Distance 3.5km **Time** 1 hour 30 **Terrain** good paths with steps, minor road **Map** OS Explorer 370 **Access** buses to Abernethy from Perth

Abernethy is a picturesque village on the very edge of Perthshire and was once home to Pictish kings. Climb the ancient round tower in the heart of the village for great views before taking a short circular around Abernethy Glen.

The village is situated on the River Earn between Bridge of Earn and Newburgh. For such a small place, Abernethy has a great deal of history and well repays a visit. Most noteworthy is the tower, one of only two remaining Irish Celtic-style round towers in Scotland, thought to date from the 11th century. You can borrow the impressively large key from the Museum of Abernethy (if it is open) and climb the spiral staircase to enjoy the wonderful view from the top. Be warned, the bell chimes on the hour and may give you a fright if you happen to be on the steep ladder beside it at the time.

Several skeletons have been unearthed from the building, leading archaeologists to speculate that it was once used as a burial place. Attached to the outer wall are medieval jougs, an iron collar and chain, remnants of a judicial system in which corporal punishment was commonplace – and public. There is also a fragment of a Pictish stone where, in 1072, Scottish king Malcolm Canmore was forced to kneel and pay homage to William the Conqueror.

Abernethy's long history as a religious centre reaches back to 460AD, with a monastery created for learning and for spreading christianity to the Picts. The

◀ Abernethy Round Tower

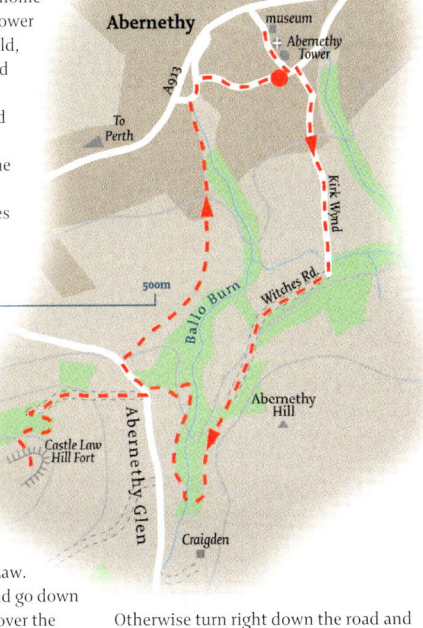

village was later selected as the home of the Pictish kings. Religious power eventually transferred to Dunkeld, though Culdee monks continued to be based here. Most of the church buildings were destroyed during the Reformation of 1560.

Cross the main square from the tower, bearing left to then turn right up Kirk Wynd, past cottages and the old church, where the narrow road soon becomes a rough track signed for Witches Road. This is named after a 'coven' of 22 local women who, according to local legend, were burnt to death on Abernethy Hill. Keep climbing, bearing left at a fork and at the next junction keep ahead to the right (signposted for Abernethy Glen circular). The path narrows as it rises by a fence on the right, with good views across the glen to Castle Law.

Continue through the trees and go down some wooden steps to a bridge over the Ballo Burn. Climb the steps on the far side and go through the kissing gate (signposted for Castlelaw and Rough Glen). At the next path junction turn left to climb up to the road. It is possible to detour from here up the path on the left to Castle Law. There is a steep climb to the remains of this hilltop Iron Age fort, but the views are superb.

Otherwise turn right down the road and leave it when a sign indicates the Rough Glen path to Abernethy on the right just beyond a bench. This was once a paved route used for transporting coal and lime from Strathmiglo. Eventually, this bears right onto a track where you descend gently to the road into Abernethy. Turn right and follow the road round to the right and then left to the village centre.

Loch Leven and Kinross House

Distance 6.5km **Time** 2 hours
Terrain excellent paths and pavement
Map OS Explorer 369 **Access** buses to Kinross from Perth and Dunfermline

This easy circuit visits the shores of Loch Leven, a fantastic spot for birdwatching, where you can also journey to an island castle by ferry before exploring Kinross.

Loch Leven is Scotland's largest Lowland loch and an important site for waterfowl, with the largest concentration of breeding ducks anywhere in the UK, as well as attracting thousands of migrating geese and swans in autumn and winter. This National Nature Reserve also has the stunning Lomond Hills for a backdrop.

Start the walk from Kinross Pier, where there is a café and summer ferry to Lochleven Castle. (Follow signs for Kirkgate Park from the centre of Kinross.) A boardwalk path to the left circumnavigates the shore of the loch and passes right through Kirkgate Park, where you then shadow the boundary wall of Kinross House. The gardens of this stately home, built by 'King's architect' William Bruce in 1685, are famous for their formal yew hedges, borders and rosebeds and are a must-see when open in summer.

Just below the stone watchtower is the castle viewpoint. It is likely that the island castle seen today is built on the site of a much older Pictish fort, although no remains have been found. According to 15th-century records, William Wallace took

part in a daring raid on the castle in 1303. It later served as a state prison, and Mary Queen of Scots was imprisoned here for almost a year in 1567. The viewpoint is also a good spot to watch the overwintering geese, more than 15,000 of which arrive every year; the sight of them flying in at sunset is spectacular.

The path soon passes the elaborate Fish Gate entrance to Kinross House. Above the gate is a carved basket of fish said to contain the seven varieties of fish that could be caught in the loch at that time – salmon, char, grey trout, speckled trout, blackhead, perch and pike. Next, you'll see a right turn to a hide set out over the water amongst the reeds, giving a chance to see whooper swans, teal, reed bunting and even ospreys in summer on Loch Leven.

Return to the main path and take a right to enter woodland. This is a sensitive habitat and dog owners are asked to keep dogs on a short lead to avoid disturbing ground-nesting birds. At a junction, bear left to follow the signed town loop, passing the golf course on the left and heading along a fine avenue of mature oak and beech trees.

Keep on the main path, bearing right through a gap in a stone wall and passing through a wooded area between housing developments. When the path reaches a road turn right and then left onto the main road near a stone building. This leads all the way back through the centre of Kinross to the clocktower, Cross Well and old town hall buildings. At a sign for Loch Leven, turn left and at the fork keep left again for Kirkgate Park. On reaching the park, bear right to return along the outward route to the pier.

◂ Castle Island from the pier on Loch Leven

Index

Aberfeldy	46
Abernethy	92
Acharn (Loch Tay)	52
Acharn Woods (Killin)	62
Allean Forest	14
Alyth	42
Amulree	76
Auchterarder	78
Ben Lawers	56
Ben Shee	80
Ben Vrackie	26
Birks of Aberfeldy	46
Birnam	36, 38
Birnam Hill	38
Black Spout	20
Blair Atholl	10, 12
Blairgowrie	40
Braan, River	30, 32
Branklyn Garden	86
Bridge of Balgie	54
Cateran Trail	42
Cargill's Leap	40
Comrie	70
Craig Varr	16
Craigower	24
Creag Bhuidhe	60
Crieff	66, 68
Deil's Cauldron	70
Drummond Hill	48
Dundurn	72
Dunkeld	30, 32, 34, 36
Earn, River	66, 92
Edramucky	56
Ericht, River	40
Falls of Bruar	8
Fingal's Stone	60
Glen Banvie	10
Glen Devon	80
Glen Lednock	70
Glen Lyon	54
Glen Quaich	76
Glen Sherup	80
Glen Tilt	12
Hermitage, The	30
Hill of Loyal	42
Killiecrankie	22
Killin	56, 58, 60, 62
Kenmore	48, 50
King's Seat (Birnam)	38
King's Seat (Dunkeld)	32
Kinloch Rannoch	16
Kinnoull Tower	86
Kinross	94
Knock, The	68
Knockie, The	40
Loch Earn	72, 74
Loch Faskally	22
Loch Freuchie	76
Loch Leven	94
Loch of the Lowes	34
Loch Rannoch	16, 18
Loch Tay	48, 50, 52, 58
Loch Tummel	14
Moncreiffe Hill	90
Moulin	24, 26
Muthill	66
Old Bridge of Tilt	10, 12
Perth	84, 86
Pitlochry	20, 22, 24, 26
Queen's View	14
Scone	88
Soldier's Leap	22
Sron a'Chlachain	60
St Fillans	72, 74
Stair Bridge	38
Strathearn	72
Tay, River	32, 36
Tummel, River	20